PARENTS' GUIDE TO TESTING

TABLE OF CONTENTS

D1317035

Parents' Guide to Testing

Introduction

Standardized achievement testing is a fact of life in public and private schools. As the United States continues moving toward applying national standards for achievement at each grade level, standardized testing will take on even greater importance to the public. Expectations for education are changing throughout the country as performance standards for students in all grades are being raised. The high-tech world of the twenty-first century will require that students acquire more sophisticated reading, writing, and math skills. Evaluation of how well the schools are helping our students meet the new national standards is the primary focus of many standardized achievement test programs.

With so much emphasis on the goal of achieving high test scores, it's not surprising that some teachers and administrators feel apprehensive when test schedules are announced. In turn, this sense of apprehension is often transmitted to their students. How can we make standardized test-taking a positive educational experience for students? Teachers and parents can familiarize themselves with the format of, the skills covered by, and the test language used in the standardized tests used in their schools. Teachers and administrators are often asked, "What's on the test?" Though specific answers to that question are not available, teachers and parents should be knowledgeable about what skills students are expected to know as they progress through school. Teachers and parents can give students the tools to assist them in improving test-taking skills. Students can be taught how to read and listen to directions, how to use an answer sheet, how to budget their time during a timed test, and even how to control test stress.

Classroom Assessments

Because teachers can use a variety of tests (multiple choice, open-ended, essay, performance tasks, observation checklists, demonstrations) and assess frequently, classroom assessments provide the most in-depth information about how well your child is meeting or exceeding standards. Classroom assessment is the most diagnostic in nature. It is also the best measure of a student's academic growth. For these reasons, the most important kind of assessment is that done in the classroom.

Student progress at the classroom level is reported through report cards and parent conferences.

District and State Assessments

Most states and local school districts also use some sort of assessments to judge student progress. These assessments vary, so contact your local school to see what sort of state and district assessments are required of students.

Norm-Referenced Tests

Norm-Referenced Tests are national tests that are written for use in any state or district. For this reason, they are not necessarily aligned with specific state or district standards.

Norm-Referenced Tests include:
- ❑ Iowa Test of Basic Skills (ITBS)
- ❑ California Achievement Test (CAT)
- ❑ Metropolitan Achievement Test (MAT)
- ❑ Preliminary Scholastic Achievement Test (PSAT)
- ❑ Scholastic Achievement Test (SAT)
- ❑ American College Test (ACT)

These national tests are "normed" using a national sample of students. They focus on skills and knowledge generally taught in a grade level across the country. Typically, such tests are multiple choice, and they measure skills or knowledge in general subject areas.

Results from these tests indicate how your child's scores compare with those of students across the nation.

Standardized Achievement Tests

Though there are many standardized tests available, the following tests administered in grades 2–6 cover the test areas of vocabulary, reading comprehension, spelling, language, mathematics, and study skills, and were selected as the basis of this test practice series. The CAT/5 is the *California Achievement Test, Fifth Edition*. The CTBS is the *Comprehensive Test of Basic Skills*. The ITBS is the *Iowa Test of Basic Skills*. The MAT/7 is the *Metropolitan Achievement Test, Seventh Edition*. The SAT is the *Stanford Achievement Test, Ninth Edition*. The TAAS is the *Texas Assessment of Academic Skills*. (TAAS is not given at grade 2.) The TerraNova is the new replacement for the CTBS and is the most recent achievement test to reach the school market.

Interpreting and Reporting Test Results

The standardized tests that elementary students frequently take are norm-referenced tests. These tests are administered in uniform testing conditions, and they compare the performance of the student to a representative sample of students from the nation's public schools. The test results are generally provided in percentile form. For example, suppose a student scores in the 68th percentile. This indicates that this student performs better than 67% of all the students in the national sample—and not as well as 32% of the students in the sample. In many school districts, parents receive standardized test results for their children either at parent conferences or through written communication. School districts often report test results by individual school for local publication in newspapers. States sometimes compare the scores of individual school districts. Standardized tests provide one measure of students' academic progress. Standardized test results are most effective when also used in conjunction with classroom assessments, which are more diagnostic in nature.

Educational Standards

In many states, educational standards have been developed. These standards are statements of what students should know and be able to do in each subject area. Standards are high and consistent expectations for all students.

This Parents' Guide to Testing lists subject areas for each grade level, with standards appropriate for that grade level. Under each standard you will find example test questions of what students should know or be able to do at that grade level.

What Is the Relationship of Performance on Standards and a Graduation Diploma?

Most states have set performance levels for certain core standards, such as reading and writing, oral communication, mathematics, and science in order for students to receive a graduation diploma. Check with your local high school to see what kind of assessment students must pass to graduate.

How Do These Standards Apply to a Child with Special Needs?

Some students are identified as having special education needs. For these special education students, the standards may be modified, accommodations may be made, or the standards might be waived, depending on the needs of the student. Special education students are expected to meet the standards written for them in their own special program.

The needs of students whose performance exceeds standards are also addressed through various program options available in local districts or schools.

How Can I Obtain More Information about Standards?

Contact your child's classroom teacher to learn more about classroom standards and your student's progress and ways in which you can provide supporting activities for your child. You may also obtain a copy of Steck-Vaughn's *Parents' Guide to Standards* (ISBN 0-8172-6184-2) at your local school supply store.

Organization

This book contains seven units, one each for Kindergarten through Grade 6. In each unit, three content areas are covered: language arts, math, and science. In each content area, six general standards are mentioned. Each general standard then includes a more specific indication of what students should know about that subject. For each specific requirement, sample test questions are included, with answers at the bottom of the page. This book does not list all the specific requirements under each general standard. The intent is simply to give parents an idea of the general standards, some specific requirements, and the sort of test questions their children might encounter in relation to these requirements. A more thorough listing of standards and specific requirements can be found in Steck-Vaughn's *Parents' Guide to Standards*.

Science is usually not included on standardized tests. This book does include sample test questions for physical science, life science, and Earth and space science for grades 1 through 6. Through an understanding of science, students can develop a better understanding of process skills.

Use

This book can be used in two ways. First, it can be used to give parents a better understanding of the test process their students encounter in the standardized testing situation. Second, it can be used as general practice in testing for students, though that is not really the intent of this book. Instead, for general testing practice, obtain a copy of Steck-Vaughn's *Test Practice*. These books are available for grades 2 through 6.

In first-grade testing, the students are usually given oral directions before they answer questions. This oral reinforcement is also used often for second-grade testing. This book includes examples of the oral directions students might receive in first-grade testing.

What Can Parents Do to Help Students Meet Standards?

Teachers work hard to educate our children. But parents must play an active role in their children's education, too. There are many things that you as parents can do to help your children gain a good education.

❏ Provide a quiet place for your child to study or do homework. Make sure your child has all the supplies necessary to complete the work.

❏ Set a time for your child to study or do homework. This will help your child to manage time better.

❏ Go over homework directions together. Make sure your child understands what he or she is supposed to do.

❏ Give help when needed, but remember that homework is your child's responsibility.

❏ Check the homework when it is done. Go over any parts your child may have had trouble completing.

❏ Help your child study for tests by asking sample questions or going over the material to be covered in the test.

❏ Review your child's schoolwork, and note improvements as well as problems.

A Final Note

Remember that standards are useless unless there is a desire to achieve them. Promote learning in your children. Help them to become better acquainted with the world around them. Encourage them to do their best in all their endeavors, both in school and outside it. Talk to your children about their lessons. Ask questions. You might even learn something new!

TESTING TERMS

Here are some terms to know concerning standardized achievement testing.

achievement test A test that measures student knowledge resulting from specific instruction.

age equivalent The score derived from age norms on a standardized test established by determining the average score made by students of each age.

age norms Typical or average performance on standardized tests for students in different age groups.

criterion-referenced test Measurement of proficiency in specific curriculum areas by evaluating a student's degree of success in completing prescribed tasks; it tells what a person is able to do.

deviation The difference between one set of values/scores and the mean.

diagnostic test A test used to discover the nature and, if possible, the causes of inability to perform average scholastic tasks.

frequency distribution A table for classifying test scores according to the number of times they occur in a group evaluation.

grade equivalent The score derived from grade norms on a standardized test.

grade norm The mean raw score obtained by students in a particular grade.

intelligence test A series of tests that measure general mental ability or scholastic aptitude.

mean The point on a scale above and below which the deviations are equal.

median The point on a scale below which half of the scores in a frequency distribution fall.

norm-referenced test A test based on standards determined by testing a large number of students of different age or grade placement; it tells how a student compares with others.

percentile rank The position assigned to a score when the scores are divided into one hundred equal divisions in descending order.

portfolio assessment This method of tracking a student's progress involves selecting chronological samples of a student's work that can be compared to show the progress over time and storing the samples in a folder.

reliability The consistency in test results; the degree to which a test's results actually measure what a student can do on a given test.

rubric A rubric is a scoring guide based on a scale for rating a group of students' papers.

standardized test A test for which norms on a reference group are provided; a test with specific procedures such that comparable measurements may be made by testers in different geographic areas.

stanine One of nine standard divisions of test scores, with the fifth stanine representing the average or mean score and a standard deviation of two.

validity The degree to which a test measures what it is designed to measure, or that it can predict performance on other measures.

"The primary purpose of . . . education is to make one's mind a pleasant place in which to spend one's time."

— Sydney J. Harris

© Steck-Vaughn Company

KINDERGARTEN

Language Arts
Math
Science

PARENTS' GUIDE TO TESTING

 # LANGUAGE ARTS

Standard 1 – Reading

Students read and understand a variety of materials.

- ❑ Connect the written word with personal experience.

- ❑ Explore language as a variety of materials are read: rhymes and poems, stories, directions, nonfiction materials, fairy tales, and folk tales.

- ❑ Begin to identify beginning, middle, and end of a story, with support and in a group.

- ❑ Begin to use word recognition strategies, with support and in a group.

- ❑ Use context clues (for example: pictures and text) while reading and being read to.

- ❑ Use information from what they have learned to develop vocabulary.

Standard 2 – Writing and Speaking

Students write and speak for a variety of purposes and audiences.

- ❑ Share personal narrative through show and tell.

- ❑ Give and receive feedback, with prompting and support, by sharing, writing, and speaking with others.

- ❑ Begin to form letters correctly with the use of manipulatives such as clay or cornmeal.

- ❑ Develop awareness of story elements, such as character, setting, problem, and solution.

Standard 3 – Language Structure

Students write and speak using conventional grammar, usage, sentence structure, punctuation, capitalization, and spelling.

- ❑ Begin to develop awareness of basic modifiers in group writing and when speaking.

- ❑ Use simple sentences to communicate thoughts and ideas when speaking.

- ❑ Differentiate between capital and lower case letters, with support.

- ❑ Use letters to represent words.

Standard 4 –Thinking and Viewing

Students apply thinking skills to their reading, writing, speaking, listening, and viewing.

❑ Practice listening skills, with support and in a group, in relation to understanding directions.

❑ Begin to use speaking and listening, in a group and with support, to define and solve problems.

❑ Begin to respond to oral presentations, in a group and with support, based on personal experience as a listener and speaker.

Standard 5 –Research

Students read to locate, select, and make use of relevant information from a variety of media, reference, and technological sources.

❑ Begin to develop appropriate questions, in a group and with support, and identify likely resources.

❑ Begin to recognize organizational features of printed text, in a group and with support (for example: title, author, and illustrator).

Standard 6 –Literature and Culture

Students read and recognize literature as a record and expression of cultural heritage.

❑ Listen to, respond to, and discuss a variety of literature.

❑ Listen to classic literature.

❑ Listen to and respond to literature, in a group and with support, related to the heritage of the United States.

 **MATH**

Standard 1 –Number Sense

Students develop number sense, use numbers and number relationships in problem-solving situations, and communicate the reasoning used in solving these problems.

❑ Read, write, compare, and order whole numbers up to 10.

❑ Explore strategies for estimation.

❑ Compare numbers less than 10 (less than, greater than).

❑ Associate numerals up to 10 with sets of objects.

Standard 2 –Patterns and Algebra

Students use algebraic methods to explore, model, and describe patterns and functions involving numbers, shapes, data, and graphs in problem-solving situations and communicate the reasoning used in solving these problems.

❑ Recognize and identify number patterns when counting by 2's, 5's, and 10's.

❑ Identify, reproduce, extend, create, and describe simple patterns and sequences involving color, shape, size, and rhythm.

❑ Correctly place data onto a simple chart or graph.

❑ Identify common characteristics of a set of objects.

❑ Place objects into appropriate sets according to common characteristics.

Standard 3 –Statistics and Probability

Students use data collection and analysis, statistics, and probability in problem-solving situations and communicate the reasoning used in solving these problems.

❑ Represent data using concrete objects.

❑ Identify relevant information.

❑ Identify more or less on a pictograph.

Boxes of Seeds Sold by Troop 312	
Flower Seeds	🌸🌸🌸🌸🌸
Vegetable Seeds	🌱🌱🌱🌱
Herb Seeds	🌿🌿🌿
Birdseed	🐦🐦

Standard 4 – Geometry

Students use geometric concepts, properties, and relationships in problem-solving situations and communicate the reasoning used in solving these problems.

❏ Identify circles, squares, rectangles, triangles, ovals, and diamonds (using familiar everyday objects, manipulatives, or pictures).

❏ Use familiar manipulatives to recognize shapes and their relationships (for example: pasta, boxes, blocks).

❏ Sort objects by size and shape.

❏ Recognize shapes of objects familiar to them in their environment (for example: circles, squares, and triangles in classroom, home, and sports).

Standard 5 – Measurement

Students use a variety of tools and techniques to measure, apply the results in problem-solving situations, and communicate the reasoning used in solving these problems.

❏ Estimate and measure length using nonstandard units (for example: hands, shoes, etc.).

❏ Compare and order objects to some attribute (for example: tallest to shortest, biggest to smallest).

❏ Demonstrate the process of measuring using a grid path.

❏ Without using measuring tools, describe the measures of familiar objects (for example: tall, taller, tallest; older, younger).

❏ Count the length of a given path, using the spaces on a grid.

Standard 6 – Computation

Students link concepts and procedures as they develop and use computational techniques, including estimation, mental arithmetic, paper and pencil, calculators, and computers, in problem-solving situations and communicate the reasoning used in solving these problems.

❑ Explore the conceptual meanings for addition and subtraction operations. (For example: If there are 8 boys and 7 girls, how many children are here today? If we have 15 children in the class and 2 are absent, how many children are here today?)

❑ Identify numbers from 1 to 20.

❑ Develop methods for estimating and computing with whole numbers by using physical models.

❑ Be exposed to the many methods that can be used for whole number calculation.

SCIENCE

Standard 1 – Scientific Investigation

Students understand the processes of scientific investigation and design as well as conduct, communicate about, and evaluate such investigations.

❑ Explore science in their environment through the use of the five senses.

❑ Use simple scientific tools (magnifying glasses, tweezers, etc.).

❑ Observe, compare, and describe structures of animals and plants.

❑ Communicate observations verbally and by drawing pictures.

Standard 2 – Physical Science

Students understand common properties, forms, and changes in matter and energy (with a focus on physics and chemistry).

- ❏ Compare objects according to different properties: size, shape, color, etc.

- ❏ Observe the sun's energy (for example: solar calculator, melting snow).

- ❏ Compare energy quantities (for example: hotter and colder).

- ❏ Describe orally or demonstrate the variety of ways that matter (objects or substances) can be put together or changed (for example: clay, paint, paper).

Standard 3 – Life Science

Students understand the characteristics and structure of living things, the processes of life, and how living things interact with each other and their environment (with a focus on biology, anatomy, physiology, botany, zoology, ecology).

- ❏ Observe, compare, and describe properties and parts of plants (root, leaf, stem).

- ❏ Study habitat, structure, and behavior of a variety of animals (fish, snails, worms, bugs).

- ❏ Distinguish between healthy and unhealthy foods.

- ❏ Observe differences in appearance of humans as they grow over time.

Standard 4 – Earth and Space Science

Students understand the processes and interactions of Earth's systems and the structure and dynamics of Earth and other objects in space (with a focus on geology, meteorology, astronomy, oceanography).

Not addressed at this level.

Standard 5 – Science, Technology, and Human Activity

Students understand interrelationships among science, technology, and human activity and how they can affect the world.

❏ Name things used in the classroom that are from the Earth (for example: water, food, soil).

❏ Distinguish between recyclable and throw-away.

❏ Identify jobs people do in the school and the tools they use.

❏ Identify ways that an individual can take care of the Earth.

Standard 6 – Scientific Connections

Students understand that science involves a particular way of knowing and understanding common connections among scientific disciplines.

❏ Perform experiments with materials to notice change.

❏ Collect data gained from direct experience (for example: pets, dogs, cats, etc.).

❏ Compare data collected with other classmates.

❏ Characterize different science explorations in which the class participates (for example: studying living vs. nonliving).

FIRST GRADE

Language Arts
Math
Science

PARENTS' GUIDE TO TESTING

© Steck-Vaughn Company

LANGUAGE ARTS

Standard 1 – Reading

Students read and understand a variety of materials.

❏ Begin to apply word recognition strategies and develop vocabulary, with support, while reading simple text and being read a variety of materials.

SAY: **In this test you will practice finding words that have the same or almost the same meaning as underlined words in sentences.**

Listen carefully. When you read a sentence you should <u>try this</u>**: look at the underlined word. Think what that word means. Then read the answer choices. Find the word that means the same or almost the same as the underlined word. Place your marker under the first sentence. This is the** <u>Sample</u>**.** *Put the flowers on the table.* **Now read the four words listed below the sentence:** *Hold, Place, See, Take.* **Darken the circle next to the word that means the same or almost the same as** *Put.*

Allow students time to choose and mark their answer. Then introduce the <u>Think It Through</u> feature.

SAY: **Now we will** <u>think it through</u>**. We will check the answer. You should have darkened the circle next to the second word,** *Place. Place* **means the same as** *Put. Hold, See,* **and** *Take* **are not correct because they do not mean the same as** *Put.*

Check to see that all students have filled in the correct answer space. Ask students if they have any questions.

SAY: **Now you will practice finding more words that mean the same or almost the same as underlined words in sentences. Do numbers 1 and 2 just as we did the** <u>Sample</u>**.**

Sample

<u>Put</u> the flowers on the table.

○ Hold
○ Place
○ See
○ Take

1. It was a <u>small</u> rabbit.

○ old
○ white
○ fat
○ little

2. JoAnn was feeling <u>scared</u>.

○ lucky
○ afraid
○ better
○ lost

Answers:
Sample Place, **1.** little, **2.** afraid

Standard 2 – Writing and Speaking

Students write and speak for a variety of purposes and audiences.

❑ Develop awareness of words (for example: introducing students to words with similar vowel sounds).

SAY: **In this test you will practice choosing words that have the same sound as underlined letters in words.**

Listen carefully. When you look at a word with an underlined letter, you should <u>try this</u>: say the sound of the letter to yourself. Think about the sound. Then find the word that has the same sound.

Place your marker under the first row, the one with the word *time*. This is the <u>Sample</u>. Look at the underlined letter in *time*. Darken the circle for the word that has the same sound as the underlined letter in *time...time*.

Allow students time to choose and mark their answer. Remind students to carefully fill in the answer space and to completely erase any stray marks. Then introduce the <u>Think It Through</u> feature.

SAY: **Now we will <u>think it through</u>. We will check the answer. You should have darkened the circle for the third word, *shine*. *Shine* has the same sound as the underlined "i" in *time*.**

Now you will practice choosing more words that have the same sound as underlined letters in words. Put your marker under the next row, the one with the word *later*. Do numbers 1 and 2 just as we did the <u>Sample</u>. Look carefully at the underlined letter. Then choose your answer from the words given in the row.

Sample

t<u>i</u>me
- ○ animal
- ○ whistle
- ○ shine
- ○ hill

1.

l<u>a</u>ter
- ○ piano
- ○ roar
- ○ arrow
- ○ grade

2.

b<u>ei</u>ng
- ○ mend
- ○ eagle
- ○ vest
- ○ web

Answers:
Sample shine, **1.** grade, **2.** eagle

Standard 3 – Language Structure

Students write and speak using conventional grammar, usage, sentence structure, punctuation, capitalization, and spelling.

❑ Begin to use correct capitalization, with support in a group, at the beginning of sentences and with proper nouns.

SAY: **Read the letter silently to yourself as I read it aloud.**

Check to see that all students find Rita's letter.

SAY: ***Dear Father,***
(1)
Are you having a fun birthday
                    (2)
I wanted to make it special.
I love you.
Your daughter,
Rita

SAY: **Now place your marker under the next row.**

Check to see that all students find item 1. Allow students time after each item to choose and mark their answer.

SAY: 1 **Look at the underlined words with the number 1 under them. How should Rita write these words? Should she write *Dear father, dear Father*, or is the group of words *Correct the way it is*? Darken the circle for *the way Rita should write the underlined words*.**

2 **Place your marker under the next row. Look at the underlined word with the number 2 under it. Which punctuation mark should Rita write at the end of this sentence? Should she write a question mark, a period, or an exclamation point? Darken the circle for *the punctuation mark Rita should write after the underlined word*.**

Dear Father,
(1)
Are you having a fun birthday
                    (2)
I wanted to make it special.

I love you.

Your daughter,
Rita

---

1. ○ Dear father,

    ○ dear Father,

    ○ Correct the way it is

---

2. ○ birthday?

    ○ birthday.

    ○ birthday!

Answers:
1. Correct the way it is, **2.** birthday?

Standard 4 – Thinking and Viewing

Students apply thinking skills to their reading, writing, speaking, listening, and viewing.

❑ Make predictions and draw conclusions, in a group and with support, about stories when being read to and reading using illustrations, title, and context clues.

SAY: **In this test, you will find sentences that tell about pictures. Place your marker under the picture in the first row. This is <u>Sample A</u>. Now look at the sentences under the picture. Darken the circle next to the sentence that tells what is happening in the picture.**

Allow students time to choose and mark their answer.

SAY: **You should have darkened the circle next to the first sentence, *The girl is watching a bird.* This sentence tells what is happening in the picture. The second sentence is not correct because it is not raining in the picture. The third sentence is not correct because the picture does not show the girl planting flowers. Only the first sentence tells about the picture.**

Check to see that all students have filled in the correct answer space. Ask students if they have any questions.

SAY: **Now you will practice finding more sentences that tell about pictures. Place your marker under the picture in the next row. Do number 1 just as we did <u>Sample A</u>. Look at each picture. Then read the sentences under the picture. Darken the circle next to the sentence that tells what is happening in the picture.**

Sample A

○ The girl is watching a bird.
○ It is raining very hard.
○ The girl is planting flowers.

1.

○ I like to march in a parade.
○ The clown rides the elephant.
○ I am having a birthday party.

Answers:
Sample A The girl is watching a bird. **1.** The clown rides the elephant.

Standard 5 – Research

Students read to locate, select, and make use of relevant information from a variety of media, reference, and technological sources.

❑ Locate appropriate resources, in a group and with support, including books and wall charts.

SAY: **Look at the picture under the title *How People Travel*. Now listen while I read you a story about Keisha. Keisha is writing a report about how people travel from place to place. She put a Table of Contents at the front of her report. Read it silently to yourself as I read it aloud. Chapter 1 is called *On Tracks* and begins on page 6. Chapter 2 is called *In Air* and begins on page 21. Chapter 3 is called *Over Land* and begins on page 38. Chapter 4 is called *By Water* and begins on page 50. Now place your marker under the next row.**

Check to see that all students find item 1. Allow students time after each item to choose and mark their answer.

SAY: 1. **Look at the Table of Contents again. Would Keisha write about ships on page 21, page 38, or page 50? Darken the circle *for the page on which Keisha would write about ships.***

2. **Place your marker under the next row on the page. Look at the Table of Contents. Would Keisha write about airplanes in chapter 1, 2, or 3? Darken the circle *for the chapter in which Keisha would write about airplanes.***

How People Travel

Table of Contents

1.   21   38   50
   ○   ○   ○

2.   1   2   3
   ○   ○   ○

Answers:
1. 50, **2.** 2

Standard 6 –Literature and Culture

Students read and recognize literature as a record and expression of cultural heritage.

❑ Listen to and, with support, read, respond to, and discuss a variety of literature.

SAY: **In this test, you will answer a question about a story that you read. Place your marker under the first row, the one that has the title, *Working with Dad*. Read the story. Then read the question and the answer choices. Darken the circle next to the correct answer.**

Allow students time to choose and mark their answer.

SAY: **You should have darkened the circle next to the third answer choice, *Planting a garden*. You can tell from the story that Terri and her dad are planting and watering seeds for a garden. The first answer choice is not correct because in the story Terri and her dad plant and water seeds, but they do not eat seeds. The second answer choice is not correct. In the last sentence Terri says that they will have good things to eat. This tells you that they were not watering flowers. The correct answer is the third answer choice.**

Working with Dad

Terri and her dad made little holes in the ground. They put a seed in each hole. Then they covered the seeds. Terri poured water on the ground. She said, "Now we will have good things to eat."

What were Terri and her dad doing?

○ Eating seeds

○ Watering flowers

○ Planting a garden

Answer:
Planting a garden

6712 MATH

Standard 1 –Number Sense

Students develop number sense, use numbers and number relationships in problem-solving situations, and communicate the reasoning used in solving these problems.

❑ Use manipulatives, a number line, and place value manipulatives to generate different representations for a given number.

SAY: **In this test, you will find pictures and numbers that answer math problems you hear. Place your marker under the first row, the one with the picture of the crayons. Now listen carefully. Darken the circle for the number that tells *exactly how many crayons are shown in the picture.***

Allow students time to choose and mark their answer.

SAY: **You should have darkened the second circle for the number *65*. There are *65* crayons shown in the picture.**

SAY: **Now you will find another picture and numbers that answer the math problem you hear. Answer this problem as you did the first one.**

Darken the circle for the number sentence that tells *how many starfish are shown in the picture.*

1.

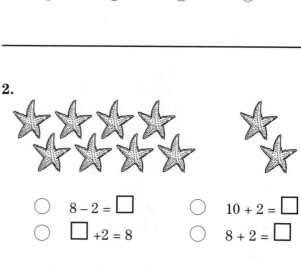

56	65	75	66
○	○	○	○

2.

○ $8 - 2 = \square$ ○ $10 + 2 = \square$

○ $\square + 2 = 8$ ○ $8 + 2 = \square$

Answers:
1. 65, **2.** $8 + 2 =$

Standard 2 – Patterns and Algebra

Students use algebraic methods to explore, model, and describe patterns and functions involving numbers, shapes, data, and graphs in problem-solving situations and communicate the reasoning used in solving these problems.

❑ Label sets according to common characteristics (for example: color, size, and shape).

SAY: **In this test you will choose pictures and numbers that answer math problems about figures and shapes.**

Listen carefully. When I read a problem, you should <u>try this</u>: look at each picture or number for the problem. Think carefully about the information in the problem. Then find the picture or number that answers the problem you hear.

SAY: 1 **Place your marker under the row, with the picture of a folded piece of paper. A shape has been cut out of this folded piece of paper. Darken the circle for the picture that shows the shape that was *cut from the paper*.**

2 **Place your marker under the next row, the one with the pattern of shapes. Be sure to move your marker so you can see the answer choices. Darken the circle for *the two shapes that come next in this pattern*.**

1.

Ⓐ   Ⓑ   Ⓒ   Ⓓ

2.

Ⓐ   Ⓑ   Ⓒ   Ⓓ

Answers:
1. C, **2.** A

Standard 3 – Statistics and Probability

Students use data collection and analysis, statistics, and probability in problem-solving situations and communicate the reasoning used in solving these problems.

❑ Record data using pictorial representations.

❑ Obtain information and relationships from graphs.

SAY: **In this test you will practice reading and answering questions about picture graphs and other math problems.**

Listen carefully. When I read a problem, you should <u>try this</u>: think carefully about the information in the problem. Then find the picture or number that answers the problem you hear.

Now we will begin. Look at the picture graph titled *Bear Sightings*. This graph shows how many bears Kim and her family saw while they were camping in a national park. Look at the sentence under the graph. This helps you to read the graph correctly. You will use this graph to answer questions 1 and 2. Now place your marker under the next row.

Check to see that all students find item 1. Allow students time after each item to choose and mark their answer. Do <u>not</u> say the item numbers.

SAY: 1   **Darken the circle for the number that tells *how many bears Kim and her family saw on Thursday, their first day at the park.***

2   **Place your marker under the next row. Darken the circle for the number that tells *which day Kim and her family saw the fewest number of bears.***

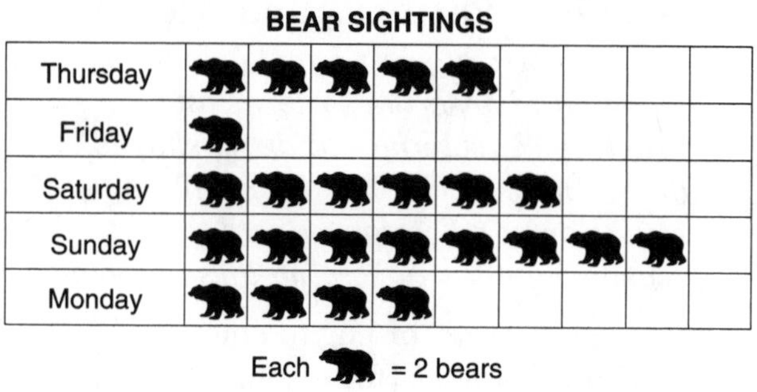

BEAR SIGHTINGS

Thursday	🐻	🐻	🐻	🐻	🐻				
Friday	🐻								
Saturday	🐻	🐻	🐻	🐻	🐻	🐻			
Sunday	🐻	🐻	🐻	🐻	🐻	🐻	🐻	🐻	
Monday	🐻	🐻	🐻	🐻	🐻				

Each 🐻 = 2 bears

1.

5	6	8	10
○	○	○	○

2.

Thursday	Friday	Saturday	Monday
○	○	○	○

Answers:
1. 10, **2.** Friday

Standard 4 –Geometry

Students use geometric concepts, properties, and relationships in problem-solving situations and communicate the reasoning used in solving these problems.

❑ Sort and classify objects by shape (using familiar everyday objects, manipulatives, or pictures).

SAY: **In this test you will practice choosing pictures that answer math problems about figures and shapes.**

Listen carefully. When I read a problem, you should <u>try this</u>: look at each picture or number for the problem. Think carefully about the information in the problem. Then find the picture or number that answers the problem you hear.

SAY: 1 **Darken the circle for the item that *is shaped like a triangle...shaped like a triangle.***
2 **Place your marker under the last row on the page. Look at the four items in the row. Darken the circle for the item that *is shaped like a rectangle.***

1.

Ⓐ   Ⓑ   Ⓒ   Ⓓ

2.

Ⓐ   Ⓑ   Ⓒ   Ⓓ

Answers:
1. D, **2.** D

Standard 5 –Measurement

Students use a variety of tools and techniques to measure, apply the results in problem-solving situations, and communicate the reasoning used in solving these problems.

❑ Estimate and measure length.

❑ Read a clock (hour intervals) and estimate time duration (how much time has passed) using standard and nonstandard units.

SAY: **In this test, you will find pictures and numbers that answer math problems you hear.**

1 **Place your marker under the row with the four clocks. Look at the clocks. Darken the circle for the clock that shows *nine o'clock...nine o'clock.***

2 **Place your marker under the last row on the page. Be sure to move your marker so you can see all of the answer choices. Look at the bus and the ruler. How long is the bus? Darken the circle for the number that tells *how long the bus is*.**

1.

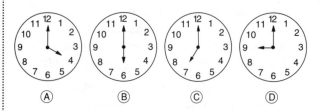

Ⓐ　　　　Ⓑ　　　　Ⓒ　　　　Ⓓ

2.

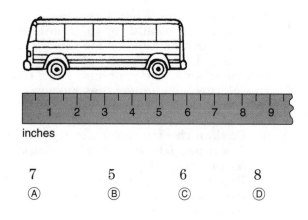

inches

7	5	6	8
Ⓐ	Ⓑ	Ⓒ	Ⓓ

Answers:
1. D, **2.** C

Standard 6 – Computation

Students link concepts and procedures as they develop and use computational techniques, including estimation, mental arithmetic, paper and pencil, calculators, and computers, in problem-solving situations and communicate the reasoning used in solving these problems.

❏ Demonstrate proficiency with basic addition facts (1-10).

SAY: **In this test, you will add numbers that answer math problems you hear or read. Place your marker under the row with the pictures of the dolls.**

Check to see that all students find item 1. Allow students time after each item to choose and mark their answer. Say each item only once. Do not say the item numbers.

SAY: 1 **Listen to this story. Mia likes rag dolls. She has been collecting rag dolls for some time. She had nine rag dolls. For her birthday she received three rag dolls. How many rag dolls does she have now? She had nine rag dolls. She received three more rag dolls. Darken the circle for the number that tells *how many rag dolls Mia has altogether.***

2 **Place your marker under the next row, the one with the pictures of the helicopter and the airplane. Ellie went to the airport. She saw six airplanes. She also saw five helicopters. Ellie saw six airplanes and five helicopters. Darken the circle for the number that tells *how many airplanes and helicopters Ellie saw at the airport.***

1.

9		15	12	6	3
3		Ⓐ	Ⓑ	Ⓒ	Ⓓ

2.

5		18	11	1	9
6		Ⓐ	Ⓑ	Ⓒ	Ⓓ

Answers:
1. B, **2.** B

SCIENCE

Standard 1 — Physical Science

Students understand common properties, forms, and changes in matter and energy (with a focus on physics and chemistry).

❑ Describe interactions that produce changes in a system: balance, stability, mixtures, etc.

Directions: Darken the circle of the correct answer to each question.

1. I pull things down to Earth. What am I?
   Ⓐ mountain
   Ⓑ glue
   Ⓒ gravity

2. You need me to lift things. What am I?
   Ⓐ force
   Ⓑ scissors
   Ⓒ gravity

3. It is easier to ride a bike
   Ⓐ upside down.
   Ⓑ up the hill.
   Ⓒ down the hill.

4. Milk is a
   Ⓐ solid.
   Ⓑ liquid.
   Ⓒ gas.

Answers:
1. C, **2.** A, **3.** C, **4.** B

Standard 2 – Life Science

Students understand the characteristics and structure of living things, the processes of life, and how living things interact with each other and their environment (with a focus on biology, anatomy, physiology, botany, zoology, ecology).

❑ Understand living vs. nonliving.

Directions: Darken the circle of the correct answer to each question.

---

1. Which of these is a living thing?
   Ⓐ cat
   Ⓑ rock
   Ⓒ bike

---

2. Which of these is not a living thing?
   Ⓐ dog
   Ⓑ tree
   Ⓒ book

3. Which of these do living things need?
   Ⓐ car
   Ⓑ food
   Ⓒ TV

---

4. Which of these is a plant?
   Ⓐ flower
   Ⓑ chicken
   Ⓒ sand

Answers:
1. A, **2.** C, **3.** B, **4.** A

Standard 4 –Earth and Space Science

Students understand the processes and interactions of Earth's systems and the structure and dynamics of Earth and other objects in space (with a focus on geology, meteorology, astronomy, oceanography).

❑ Identify changes in weather.

Directions: Darken the circle of the correct answer to each question.

---

1. Moving air is called
   Ⓐ soil.
   Ⓑ wind.
   Ⓒ thunder.

---

2. We get heat and light from the
   Ⓐ North Pole.
   Ⓑ Moon.
   Ⓒ Sun.

3. Rain comes from
   Ⓐ the Sun.
   Ⓑ the Moon.
   Ⓒ clouds.

---

4. Clouds look ___ when it rains.
   Ⓐ dark
   Ⓑ funny
   Ⓒ short

Answers:
1. B, **2.** C, **3.** C, **4.** A

SECOND GRADE

Language Arts
Math
Science

PARENTS' GUIDE TO TESTING

LANGUAGE ARTS

Standard 1 –Reading

Students read and understand a variety of materials.

❑ Apply word recognition strategies when reading a variety of materials: rhymes and poems, stories, directions, nonfiction material, fairy tales and folk tales, including those from other communities and cultures.

Directions: For questions 1–4 read both sentences. Then darken the circle for the word that fits both sentences.

1. We are learning how to put words in A, B, C _____.
   I want to _____ the new magazine.
   Ⓐ buy
   Ⓑ read
   Ⓒ order
   Ⓓ fold

2. Please _____ me that book.
   What does the minute _____ on the clock say?
   Ⓐ give
   Ⓑ sell
   Ⓒ find
   Ⓓ hand

3. I'll plant a new flower _____ next spring.
   My mother bought a new quilt for my _____ .
   Ⓐ row
   Ⓑ chair
   Ⓒ bed
   Ⓓ watch

4. Did you hear the phone _____?
   Draw a _____ around the correct answer.
   Ⓐ bell
   Ⓑ ring
   Ⓒ line
   Ⓓ call

Answers:
1. C, **2.** D, **3.** C, **4.** B

Standard 2 – Writing and Speaking

Students write and speak for a variety of purposes and audiences.

❑ Begin using descriptive vocabulary and, with support, begin to use figures of speech to communicate a clear message.

Directions: For questions 1–3 read the poem. Then darken the circle for the correct answer.

A Flower Grows

First a seed so tiny
    Hidden from our sight;
Then two tiny little leaves
    Looking for the light;

Soon a bud appears
    And then a pretty flower,
Touched by golden sunshine,
    Washed by a silver shower;

Growing prettier and prettier,
    Hour by hour!
Touched by golden sunshine,
    Washed by a silver shower.

1. What metal does the poet use to describe rain?
   Ⓐ gold
   Ⓑ tin
   Ⓒ silver
   Ⓓ brass

2. What are the tiny leaves trying to do?
   Ⓐ look for light
   Ⓑ turn into flowers
   Ⓒ grow prettier
   Ⓓ touch the golden sunshine

3. Why is the seed hidden from sight?
   Ⓐ It is very tiny.
   Ⓑ It is looking for light.
   Ⓒ It is planted in soil.
   Ⓓ It is washed by silver showers.

Answers:
1. C, 2. A, 3. C

Standard 3 – Language Structure

Students write and speak using conventional grammar, usage, sentence structure, punctuation, capitalization, and spelling.

❑ Begin to use correct basic capitalization and basic ending punctuation of simple sentences.

Directions: For numbers 1–2 darken the circle next to the sentence that has correct punctuation and capitalization.

1. Ⓐ May I help you
   Ⓑ I would like to go for a walk
   Ⓒ she is not home yet
   Ⓓ Where did you go yesterday?

2. Ⓐ Kate and I will come with you.
   Ⓑ How is your grandmother feeling
   Ⓒ Have you ever been to Florida
   Ⓓ This is My new coat.

Standard 4 – Thinking and Viewing

Students apply thinking skills to their reading, writing, speaking, listening, and viewing.

❑ Begin to recognize author's point of view, in a group and with support.

Directions: For question 3 read the paragraph. Then darken the circle for the correct answer to the question.

Some moths are as beautiful as butterflies. One very pretty moth is the Luna moth. "Luna" was the name of the Roman goddess of the Moon. The Luna moth has pretty, pale green wings that end in two long, thin tails behind. There is a pink spot on each lower wing.

3. You can tell that the author of this article thinks ___.
   Ⓐ moths can be as beautiful as butterflies
   Ⓑ moths are pests
   Ⓒ we should watch caterpillars spin cocoons
   Ⓓ moths have tails

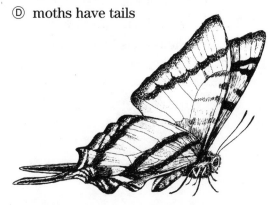

Answers:
1. D, 2. A, 3. A

Standard 5 –Research

Students read to locate, select, and make use of relevant information from a variety of media, reference, and technological sources.

❑ Recognize organizational features of printed text (for example: title, author, illustrator, title page, page numbering, table of contents, structure of text, index, chapter headings, copyright information, alphabetizing) and some features of electronic media.

Directions: For questions 1–4 read the table of contents. Then darken the circle by the correct answer to each question.

Contents

1. From this table of contents, you can tell that this is a book about ____ .
   Ⓐ sports
   Ⓑ fairy tales
   Ⓒ nature

2. How many chapters does this book have about animals and birds?
   Ⓐ 5
   Ⓑ 3
   Ⓒ 4

3. On which page does the chapter about rabbits start?
   Ⓐ 22
   Ⓑ 46
   Ⓒ 1

4. On which page does the chapter about pigeons end?
   Ⓐ 21
   Ⓑ 12
   Ⓒ 34

Answers:
1. C, **2.** A, **3.** B, **4.** A

Standard 6 –Literature and Culture

Students read and recognize literature as a record and expression of cultural heritage.

❑ Read, respond to, and discuss a variety of literature (for example: fiction, rhymes and poems, nonfiction).

Directions: For questions 1–3 read the poem. Then darken the circle for the correct answer to each question.

The Animal Fair

We went to the animal fair.
The birds and the bees were there.
The big baboon by the light of
  the Moon
Was combing his auburn hair.
The monkey smelled a skunk
And sat on the elephant's trunk.
The elephant sneezed and fell on
  his knees,
So what became of the monk ...
  the monk ... the monk?

1. What was the baboon doing?
   Ⓐ He was eating a banana.
   Ⓑ He was combing his hair.
   Ⓒ He was sneezing.
   Ⓓ He was sitting on the Moon.

2. Why did the elephant fall?
   Ⓐ He sneezed.
   Ⓑ The bee stung him.
   Ⓒ He didn't like the monkey.
   Ⓓ The birds were there.

3. What do you think the monkey did?
   Ⓐ He cooked dinner.
   Ⓑ He went shopping.
   Ⓒ He ran away.
   Ⓓ He read a book.

Answers:
1. B, **2.** A, **3.** C

 MATH

Standard 1 –Number Sense

Students develop number sense, use numbers and number relationships in problem-solving situations, and communicate the reasoning used in solving these problems.

❑ Read, name, count, and order time in intervals of minutes, hours, days, months, and years.

> **Directions:** For questions 1–3 darken the circle for the correct answer to each question. Use the calendar for question 1.

1. What day of the week is November 18?

   Ⓐ Wednesday
   Ⓑ Thursday
   Ⓒ Friday
   Ⓓ Saturday

\multicolumn{7}{c}{November}
Sun	Mon	Tues	Wed	Thur	Fri	Sat
			1	2	3	4
5	6	7	8	9	10	11
12	13	14	15	16	17	18
19	20	21	22	23	24	25
26	27	28	29	30		

2. What time is it?

   Ⓐ 3:00
   Ⓑ 3:05
   Ⓒ 1:15
   Ⓓ 2:15

3. How many inches high is this stack of books?

   Ⓐ 20 inches
   Ⓑ 5 inches
   Ⓒ 10 inches
   Ⓓ 15 inches

Standard 2 –Patterns and Algebra

Students use algebraic methods to explore, model, and describe patterns and functions involving numbers, shapes, data, and graphs in problem-solving situations and communicate the reasoning used in solving these problems.

❑ Identify, reproduce, extend, create, and describe more complex patterns and sequences involving color, shape, size, and number.

> **Directions:** For questions 4-5 darken the circle for the correct answer to each question.

4. Which figure fits next in this pattern?

   Ⓐ A
   Ⓑ B
   Ⓒ C

   □△□○□△ **?**

   △   ○   □
   A   **B**   **C**

5. Which group of numbers is missing from the pattern?

8, 10, 12 ___, ___, ___, 20

   Ⓐ 13, 14, 15
   Ⓑ 2, 4, 6
   Ⓒ 14, 16, 18
   Ⓓ 22, 24, 26

> **Answers:**
> **1.** D, **2.** D, **3.** C, **4.** C, **5.** C

Standard 3 –Statistics and Probability

Students use data collection and analysis, statistics, and probability in problem-solving situations and communicate the reasoning used in solving these problems.

❑ Given data displayed in different kinds of graphs, determine greatest and least, greater than and less than.

Directions: For question 1 study the graph. Then darken the circle for the correct answer to the question.

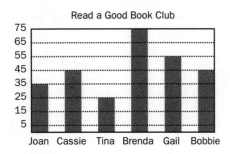

1. Who read the most books?

   Ⓐ Cassie

   Ⓑ Joan

   Ⓒ Brenda

   Ⓓ Gail

Standard 4 –Geometry

Students use geometric concepts, properties, and relationships in problem-solving situations and communicate the reasoning used in solving these problems.

❑ Classify various two-dimensional geometric shapes according to given attributes (using everyday objects, manipulatives, or pictures).

Directions: For questions 2–5 darken the circle for the correct answer to each question.

2. Which figure has 4 triangles?

   Ⓐ A

   Ⓑ B

   Ⓒ C

   Ⓓ D

   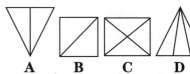

3. Which of these has a square in a circle?

   Ⓐ A

   Ⓑ B

   Ⓒ C

4. How many sides are in this figure?

   Ⓐ 6

   Ⓑ 8

   Ⓒ 10

   Ⓓ 5

5. Which of these has a triangle in a circle?

   Ⓐ A

   Ⓑ B

   Ⓒ C

Answers:
1. C, **2.** C, **3.** C, **4.** B, **5.** C

Standard 5 –Measurement

Students use a variety of tools and techniques to measure, apply the results in problem-solving situations, and communicate the reasoning used in solving these problems.

❑ Demonstrate the process of measuring length, time, and money, given the appropriate tools.

Directions: For questions 1–2 darken the circle for the correct answer to each question.

1. Which one of these shows the time on the round clock?

   Ⓐ A
   Ⓑ B
   Ⓒ C

   A 5:00

   B 8:00

   C 3:00

2. Kay has 80¢. If she buys a flower, how much money will she have left?

   Ⓐ 10¢
   Ⓑ 30¢
   Ⓒ 5¢
   Ⓓ 20¢

   50¢

Standard 6 –Computation

Students link concepts and procedures as they develop and use computational techniques, including estimation, mental arithmetic, paper and pencil, calculators, and computers, in problem-solving situations and communicate the reasoning used in solving these problems.

❑ Demonstrate conceptual meaning and proficiency with basic addition and subtraction facts (for example: 2 digit without regrouping).

Directions: For questions 3–4 darken the circle by the correct answer to the problems.

3.   49
   + 50
   ―――

   Ⓐ 100
   Ⓑ 99
   Ⓒ 199
   Ⓓ 90

4.   92
   – 41
   ―――

   Ⓐ 41
   Ⓑ 51
   Ⓒ 42
   Ⓓ 29

Answers:
1. A, **2.** B, **3.** B, **4.** B

🪐 SCIENCE

Standard 1 –Physical Science

Students understand common properties, forms, and changes in matter and energy (with a focus on physics and chemistry).

❏ Know that objects can be described and classified by their composition and physical properties.

Directions: Darken the circle of the correct answer to each question.

1. Solids have weight and
   Ⓐ shape.
   Ⓑ air.
   Ⓒ tools.
   Ⓓ liquid.

2. Water is a
   Ⓐ solid.
   Ⓑ liquid.
   Ⓒ gas.
   Ⓓ magnet.

3. Heavy things are ___ to lift.
   Ⓐ easy
   Ⓑ fun
   Ⓒ hard
   Ⓓ sad

4. A rock is a
   Ⓐ liquid.
   Ⓑ gas.
   Ⓒ solid.
   Ⓓ box.

Answers:
1. A, **2.** B, **3.** C, **4.** C

Standard 2 –Life Science

Students understand the characteristics and structure of living things, the processes of life, and how living things interact with each other and their environment (with a focus on biology, anatomy, physiology, botany, zoology, ecology).

❑ Compare the lifestyles of various plants and animals: habitats, place in the food chain, who eats them, whom they eat.

Directions: Darken the circle of the correct answer to each question.

1. The natural home of a plant or animal is called a
   Ⓐ forest.
   Ⓑ habitat.
   Ⓒ shelter.
   Ⓓ house.

2. Everything around a living thing is its
   Ⓐ environment.
   Ⓑ animal.
   Ⓒ ocean.
   Ⓓ enemy.

3. Plants and animals ___ with each other in their environments.
   Ⓐ play
   Ⓑ study
   Ⓒ interact
   Ⓓ dance

4. A plant uses air, water, and ___ to make food.
   Ⓐ animals
   Ⓑ sunlight
   Ⓒ money
   Ⓓ tools

Answers:
1. B, 2. A, 3. C, 4. B

Standard 3 –Earth and Space Science

Students understand the processes and interactions of Earth's systems and the structure and dynamics of Earth and other objects in space (with a focus on geology, meteorology, astronomy, oceanography).

❑ Identify uses of rocks and soils.

❑ Recognize that fossils are evidence of past life.

❑ Know that Earth materials consist of solid rocks, soils, liquid water, and the gases of the atmosphere.

❑ Investigate properties of clay and soil.

Directions: Darken the circle of the correct answer to each question.

1. Most of the Earth is covered by
   Ⓐ water.
   Ⓑ woods.
   Ⓒ grass.
   Ⓓ houses.

2. Land is made of soil and
   Ⓐ Sun.
   Ⓑ air.
   Ⓒ rock.
   Ⓓ wind.

3. Air is an invisible
   Ⓐ rock.
   Ⓑ gas.
   Ⓒ solid.
   Ⓓ liquid.

4. ____ are made of tiny drops of water.
   Ⓐ Volcanoes
   Ⓑ Rocks
   Ⓒ Clouds
   Ⓓ Stars

Answers:
1. A, **2.** C, **3.** B, **4.** C

THIRD GRADE

Language Arts
Math
Science

PARENTS' GUIDE TO TESTING

LANGUAGE ARTS

Standard 1 –Reading

Students read and understand a variety of materials.

❑ Use comprehension strategies, with support (including comparing/contrasting, developing awareness of text structure, identifying author's purpose or main idea, inferring, predicting, previewing, summarizing, recognizing the use of figures of speech, re-reading, and researching new material).

Directions: For questions 1–3 read the story. Then darken the circle for the correct answer.

One morning there was frost. Little white splinters of ice stuck to every green blade, every leaf, and every plant in the garden. That very day the leaves on the tomatoes, beans, and other plants in the garden withered and turned black. The leaves on the tree had already begun to turn yellow and red. Now they changed much faster. It seemed almost like a yellow and red world.

1. What season is this story about?
   Ⓐ summer
   Ⓑ fall
   Ⓒ winter
   Ⓓ spring

2. What is another word for *withered*?
   Ⓐ wintered
   Ⓑ tore
   Ⓒ slipped
   Ⓓ dried

3. What made the plants turn black?
   Ⓐ the frost
   Ⓑ the green blades
   Ⓒ the yellow and red leaves
   Ⓓ the early morning

Answers:
1. B, **2.** D, **3.** A

Standard 2 –Writing and Speaking

Students write and speak for a variety of purposes and audiences.

❑ Continue to develop awareness of homonyms, antonyms, and synonyms.

Directions: For questions 1–3 look for the word that means the same or almost the same as the underlined word. Then darken the circle for the correct answer.

1. huge
   Ⓐ large
   Ⓑ tree
   Ⓒ strong
   Ⓓ building

2. injure
   Ⓐ just
   Ⓑ journey
   Ⓒ hurt
   Ⓓ help

3. above
   Ⓐ road
   Ⓑ walk
   Ⓒ threw
   Ⓓ over

Standard 3 –Language Structure

Students write and speak using conventional grammar, usage, sentence structure, punctuation, capitalization, and spelling.

❑ Use root words, prefixes, and suffixes.

Directions: For questions 4–5 read the underlined word. Look for the prefix or the suffix. Then darken the circle for the correct answer.

4. Find the prefix of the underlined word.
   review
   Ⓐ rev
   Ⓑ view
   Ⓒ re
   Ⓓ revi

5. Find the suffix of the underlined word.
   wonderful
   Ⓐ ful
   Ⓑ wonder
   Ⓒ won
   Ⓓ der

Answers:
1. A, **2.** C, **3.** D, **4.** C, **5.** A

Standard 4 –Thinking and Viewing

Students apply thinking skills to their reading, writing, speaking, listening, and viewing.

❑ Begin to predict and draw conclusions about stories using illustrations, title, context, captions, chapter headings.

Directions: For questions 1–2 decide which sentence tells about the picture. Then darken the circle for the correct answer.

1.

Ⓐ The girls are going for a walk.

Ⓑ The girls are dancing to the radio music.

Ⓒ The girls are in school.

Ⓓ The girls are jogging in the park.

2.

Ⓐ The puppy is running away from the boy.

Ⓑ The boy doesn't want the puppy to come to him.

Ⓒ The puppy is jumping on the boy's lap.

Ⓓ The boy wants the puppy to run to him.

Standard 5 –Research

Students read to locate, select, and make use of relevant information from a variety of media, reference, and technological sources.

❑ Alphabetize to the third letter as an aid in locating information.

Directions: Darken the circle for the correct answer.

3. Which of these words would you find on a dictionary page with the guide words *globe* and *gobble*?

Ⓐ gold

Ⓑ goods

Ⓒ glow

Ⓓ gone

Answers:
1. B, **2.** D, **3.** C

Standard 6 –Literature and Culture

Students read and recognize literature as a record and expression of cultural heritage.

❑ Begin to read, respond to, and discuss, in a group and with support, literature related to the heritage of the United States.

> **Directions:** For questions 1–3 read the story. Then darken the circle for the correct answer.

Getting enough drinking water and water to put out fires was a serious problem for the people of New York City in 1774. "Tea Water" men had licenses to cart and sell water from pure springs to people in the city, but this wasn't enough water.

A man named Christopher Colles came up with a plan for a waterworks. His idea was to build a covered reservoir, or artificial lake, to store water. From the reservoir he wanted to send pure water through thirteen miles of hollowed-out log pipes. His plan was to convey water to every street and lane in New York City with pipes placed every one hundred yards. Mr. Colles assured everyone that they would be able to draw water at any time of day or night.

The plan was for the water pump to pump two hundred gallons of water at a rate of fifty-two feet per minute. The city agreed to follow this plan, but before work could be started, the Revolutionary War broke out and the need for clean water was forgotten for a while.

1. What problem did the people of New York City have?
   - Ⓐ building water pumps
   - Ⓑ licensing "Tea Water" men
   - Ⓒ getting pure drinking water
   - Ⓓ building a reservoir

2. How did the people of New York City get clean drinking water in 1774?
   - Ⓐ They pumped it from pure springs.
   - Ⓑ They bought it from "Tea Water" men.
   - Ⓒ They built a huge pump.
   - Ⓓ They covered the reservoir.

3. What does the word *convey* mean in this story?
   - Ⓐ lift
   - Ⓑ drink
   - Ⓒ pure
   - Ⓓ carry

Answers:
1. C, **2.** B, **3.** D

 MATH

Standard 1 – Number Sense

Students develop number sense, use numbers and number relationships in problem-solving situations, and communicate the reasoning used in solving these problems.

❑ Use estimation for mental arithmetic in addition and subtraction.

Directions: For questions 1–4 darken the circle for the correct answer.

---

1. Which is the closest estimate of $879 – $410?
   Ⓐ $900 – $400
   Ⓑ $800 – $400
   Ⓒ $800 – $500
   Ⓓ $700 – $400

2. Mrs. Stellato wants to buy both of these T-shirts. What is the best estimate of how much the shirts will cost?
   Ⓐ $40
   Ⓑ $20
   Ⓒ $30
   Ⓓ $15

3. Which is the best estimate of the temperature of a cup of hot chocolate?
   Ⓐ 110° F
   Ⓑ 22° F
   Ⓒ 60° F
   Ⓓ 75° F

4. Which of the following would you use to estimate 63 plus 22?
   Ⓐ 70 and 20
   Ⓑ 70 and 30
   Ⓒ 60 and 20
   Ⓓ 60 and 30

Answers:
1. A, **2.** C, **3.** A, **4.** C

Standard 2 –Patterns and Algebra

Students use algebraic methods to explore, model, and describe patterns and functions involving numbers, shapes, data, and graphs in problem-solving situations and communicate the reasoning used in solving these problems.

❑ Identify, reproduce, extend, create, and describe simple patterns and sequences involving whole numbers, negative numbers, fractions, and decimals.

Directions: For questions 1–2 darken the circle for the correct answer.

1. Which number is missing in this pattern?

   10, 12, ___, 16, 18
   - Ⓐ 13
   - Ⓑ 14
   - Ⓒ 15
   - Ⓓ 12

2. How many hearts should there be in the next square?

   - Ⓐ 8
   - Ⓑ 9
   - Ⓒ 6
   - Ⓓ 5

Standard 3 –Statistics and Probability

Students use data collection and analysis, statistics, and probability in problem-solving situations and communicate the reasoning used in solving these problems.

❑ Construct, read, and interpret displays of data including tables, charts, pictographs, and bar graphs.

Directions: Use this chart to answer question 3.

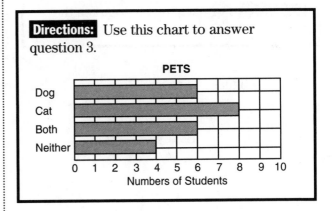

3. How many students have both cats and dogs?
   - Ⓐ 8
   - Ⓑ 7
   - Ⓒ 6
   - Ⓓ Not given

Answers:
1. B, **2.** B, **3.** C

Standard 4 –Geometry

Students use geometric concepts, properties, and relationships in problem-solving situations and communicate the reasoning used in solving these problems.

❑ Identify circular, triangular, square, and rectangular objects and recreate their shapes.

Directions: For questions 1–4 darken the circle for the correct answer.

1. Which figure is a square?

Ⓐ A
Ⓑ B
Ⓒ C
Ⓓ D

2. Which of these figures is all rectangles?

Ⓐ A
Ⓑ B
Ⓒ C
Ⓓ D

3. Which symbol belongs in the blank space?

Ⓐ star
Ⓑ square
Ⓒ triangle
Ⓓ circle

4. Which figure shows a line of symmetry?

Ⓐ A
Ⓑ B
Ⓒ C
Ⓓ D

Answers:
1. B, **2.** D, **3.** C, **4.** A

Standard 5 – Measurement

Students use a variety of tools and techniques to measure, apply the results in problem-solving situations, and communicate the reasoning used in solving these problems.

❑ Estimate and measure length, perimeter, time (5 minute intervals), and capacity (pints, cups, quarts, and gallons) using standard units, with an understanding of the results.

Directions: For questions 1–2 darken the circle for the correct answer.

1. What is the perimeter of this polygon?

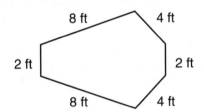

Ⓐ 28 feet

Ⓑ 18 feet

Ⓒ 20 feet

Ⓓ 10 feet

2. Vera leaves home at 9:00 a.m. every day. It takes her 15 minutes to walk to school. Which clock shows the time she gets to school?

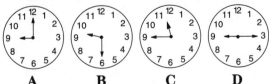

   A   B   C   D

Ⓐ A

Ⓑ B

Ⓒ C

Ⓓ D

Standard 6 – Computation

Students link concepts and procedures as they develop and use computational techniques, including estimation, mental arithmetic, paper and pencil, calculators, and computers, in problem-solving situations and communicate the reasoning used in solving these problems.

❑ Select and use appropriate methods for computing with whole numbers in problem-solving situations from among mental arithmetic, estimation, paper-and-pencil algorithms, and calculator or other mechanical methods in addition, subtraction, and multiplication.

Directions: For questions 3–4 darken the circle for the correct answer.

3. Which number sentence can you use to check the answer to this number sentence?

$16 - 9 = 7$

Ⓐ $9 + 9 = 18$

Ⓑ $16 + 9 = 25$

Ⓒ $9 + 7 = 16$

Ⓓ $9 - 7 = 2$

4. Kyle saved $5.00 to buy a present for his mother. The present he wants to buy costs $12.00. How much more money does Kyle need?

Ⓐ $17.00

Ⓑ $7.00

Ⓒ $2.00

Ⓓ $10.00

Answers:
1. A, **2.** D, **3.** C, **4.** B

🪐 SCIENCE

Standard 1 –Physical Science

Students understand common properties, forms, and changes in matter and energy (with a focus on physics and chemistry).

❑ Explore mechanical energy.

Directions: For questions 1-5 darken the circle for the correct answer. Use the picture to answer questions 2, 3, and 4.

---

1. Work is done when
   - Ⓐ a force is used.
   - Ⓑ a force moves an object
   - Ⓒ nothing moves.
   - Ⓓ a person holds something.

2. What machine is being used in the picture?
   - Ⓐ inclined plane
   - Ⓑ lever
   - Ⓒ screw
   - Ⓓ wedge

3. Another name for this machine is a
   - Ⓐ spring scale.
   - Ⓑ ramp.
   - Ⓒ lever.
   - Ⓓ wheel.

4. This machine makes work easier because it
   - Ⓐ has a sharp point.
   - Ⓑ has a slanted surface.
   - Ⓒ moves slowly.
   - Ⓓ moves quickly.

5. An inclined plane that winds around a spiral is
   - Ⓐ a lever.
   - Ⓑ a wedge.
   - Ⓒ a screw.
   - Ⓓ an ax.

Answers:
1. B, **2.** A, **3.** B, **4.** B, **5.** C

Standard 2 – Life Science

Students understand the characteristics and structure of living things, the processes of life, and how living things interact with each other and their environment (with a focus on biology, anatomy, physiology, botany, zoology, ecology).

❑ Investigate basic needs and traits of plants and animals.

Directions: For questions 1-5 darken the circle for the correct answer.

1. Features that living things have are called
   Ⓐ faces.
   Ⓑ traits.
   Ⓒ groups.
   Ⓓ chains.

2. Both plants and animals have
   Ⓐ stems.
   Ⓑ noses.
   Ⓒ cells.
   Ⓓ houses.

3. Giving birth to live young and having fur are traits of
   Ⓐ mammals.
   Ⓑ plants.
   Ⓒ insects.
   Ⓓ reptiles.

4. Behaviors that do not have to be learned are
   Ⓐ camouflage.
   Ⓑ defense.
   Ⓒ instincts.
   Ⓓ insects.

5. The green material in plants is
   Ⓐ water.
   Ⓑ paint.
   Ⓒ sunlight.
   Ⓓ chlorophyll.

Answers:
1. B, **2.** C, **3.** A, **4.** C, **5.** D

Standard 3 –Earth and Space Science

Students understand the processes and interactions of Earth's systems and the structure and dynamics of Earth and other objects in space (with a focus on geology, meteorology, astronomy, oceanography).

❑ Identify basic components of our solar system.

Directions: For questions 1-5 darken the circle for the correct answer.

1. Each planet in the solar system travels around the
   - Ⓐ Moon.
   - Ⓑ Sun.
   - Ⓒ Earth.
   - Ⓓ comets.

2. Each planet travels in a path called
   - Ⓐ an orbit.
   - Ⓑ a solar system.
   - Ⓒ a galaxy.
   - Ⓓ a satellite.

3. The closest planet to the Sun is
   - Ⓐ Mercury.
   - Ⓑ Venus.
   - Ⓒ Earth.
   - Ⓓ Mars.

4. The pull that keeps us on Earth is
   - Ⓐ friction.
   - Ⓑ magnetism.
   - Ⓒ gravity.
   - Ⓓ sunlight.

5. In a solar eclipse, the Moon moves between ___ and the Sun.
   - Ⓐ Venus.
   - Ⓑ the Earth.
   - Ⓒ the North Star.
   - Ⓓ the Milky Way.

Answers:
1. B, 2. A, 3. A, 4. C, 5. B

FOURTH GRADE

Language Arts
Math
Science

PARENTS' GUIDE TO TESTING

LANGUAGE ARTS

Standard 1 – Reading

Students read and understand a variety of materials.

❑ Apply word recognition strategies when reading a variety of materials: rhymes and poems, stories, directions, nonfiction material, fairy tales, and folk tales, including those from other communities and cultures.

> **Directions:** For questions 1–4 read the selection. Then darken the circle for the correct answer to each question.

Although geckos are small lizards, not plants, they grow buds after they shed their tails. Geckos can shed their tails when they are attacked. When a gecko's tail drops off, it continues to wriggle on the ground. The attacker can be confused by the wriggling tail. This gives the gecko time to escape. Soon new cells grow in the place where the old tail had been. These cells are called buds. It takes about eight to twelve months for a gecko to grow a new, full-sized tail.

1. What does the word *shed* mean in this selection?
   Ⓐ cast off
   Ⓑ hut
   Ⓒ old building
   Ⓓ grow out

2. What is this selection mainly about?
   Ⓐ different kinds of buds
   Ⓑ what a gecko is
   Ⓒ how geckos protect themselves
   Ⓓ making tails wriggle

3. How long does it take for the gecko to grow a new tail?
   Ⓐ eight months
   Ⓑ twelve months
   Ⓒ a year
   Ⓓ between eight and twelve months

4. What are geckos?
   Ⓐ lizards
   Ⓑ plants
   Ⓒ buds
   Ⓓ tails

Answers:
1. A, **2.** C, **3.** D, **4.** A

Standard 2 – Writing and Speaking

Students write and speak for a variety of purposes (expository, persuasive, narrative, and creative writing) and audiences.

❏ Use character, setting, and plot sequence events appropriately.

Directions: For questions 1–4 darken the circle for the sentence that best answers the question.

---

1. Rose is reading a book called *Spinning on Ice.*
   Which of these is probably the last sentence in the book?
   Ⓐ Tanya laced her skates and went out on the ice.
   Ⓑ Tanya's costume glittered in the spotlight.
   Ⓒ Tanya could hear the applause as she skated off the ice.
   Ⓓ Tanya looked for her parents in the audience.

2. Which of these sentences would probably come after the following?
   Mother opened the door quietly. On the table was a beautiful birthday cake.
   Ⓐ The room was very clean.
   Ⓑ The children were watching TV.
   Ⓒ Everyone shouted, "Surprise!"
   Ⓓ The kitten was asleep on the windowsill.

3. Which of these sentences would probably come after the following?
   Joella thought of a way she could help her mother feel better.
   Ⓐ Then she had an argument with her big brother.
   Ⓑ She decided to go to the movies.
   Ⓒ She sat down to watch her favorite TV show.
   Ⓓ She straightened up the house and prepared dinner.

4. Luis is reading a book called *Candy and Me.* Which of these might be the last sentence in the book?
   Ⓐ Then Fred emptied his "Trick or Treat" bag onto the table.
   Ⓑ They only had two more streets to go.
   Ⓒ The bag was really getting full.
   Ⓓ He wondered what the new neighbors would give him.

Answers:
1. C, **2.** C, **3.** D, **4.** A

Standard 3 –Language Structure

Students write and speak using conventional grammar, usage, sentence structure, punctuation, capitalization, and spelling.

❑ Identify some parts of speech, such as nouns, verbs, and adjectives.

Directions: For questions 1–2 darken the circle for the simple subject.

1. <u>Janet</u> <u>is</u> my <u>older</u> <u>sister</u>.
   Ⓐ Ⓑ   Ⓒ   Ⓓ

2. <u>We</u> <u>danced</u> and sang at <u>Arthur's</u> <u>party</u>.
   Ⓐ   Ⓑ   Ⓒ   Ⓓ

Directions: For questions 3–4 darken the circle for the simple predicate.

3. <u>Roger</u> <u>is</u> my <u>older</u> <u>brother</u>.
   Ⓐ   Ⓑ   Ⓒ   Ⓓ

4. <u>Randy</u> <u>collects</u> rare <u>old</u> <u>coins</u>.
   Ⓐ   Ⓑ   Ⓒ Ⓓ

Standard 4 –Thinking and Viewing

Students apply thinking skills to their reading, writing, speaking, listening, and viewing.

❑ Formulate questions about what they read, write, hear, and view.

Directions: For questions 5–6 read the paragraph. Then answer the questions.

(**1**) The donkey and the ox were two of the first animals to be used as pack animals. (**2**) Pack animals are still used in less-developed countries today. (**3**) They are especially useful where there are no modern roads. (**4**) Horses can travel in the mountains.

5. Which sentence does not belong in this paragraph?
   Ⓐ Sentence 1
   Ⓑ Sentence 2
   Ⓒ Sentence 3
   Ⓓ Sentence 4

6. Which would be a good opening sentence for this paragraph?
   Ⓐ Some countries are less developed than the U.S.
   Ⓑ Farmers have to drag a lot of equipment.
   Ⓒ Pack animals can carry more than people can carry.
   Ⓓ Long ago, people started using pack animals to carry heavy loads.

Answers:
1. A, **2.** A, **3.** B, **4.** B, **5.** D, **6.** D

Standard 5 – Research

Students read to locate, select, and make use of relevant information from a variety of media, reference, and technological sources.

❏ Sort information as it relates to a specific topic or purpose.

> **Directions:** Study this outline for a research report. Then answer questions 1–3.

Transportation Through the Ages

I. Early ways of travel
   A. Foot
   B. Pack animal
   C. _____

II. The beginning of mass transportation
   A. Steamship
   B. _____

III. _____
   A. Automobiles
   B. Airplanes
   C. Spaceships

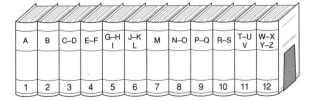

1. Which one of these topics would fit best on line I, C?
   Ⓐ Bus
   Ⓑ Wagon
   Ⓒ Automobile
   Ⓓ Steamship

2. Which topic would fit on line II, B?
   Ⓐ Wagon
   Ⓑ Animal
   Ⓒ Railroad
   Ⓓ Airship

3. What is a good heading for III?
   Ⓐ Transportation today
   Ⓑ Modern steamship travel
   Ⓒ Space exploration
   Ⓓ New kinds of planes

Answers:
1. B, 2. C, 3. A

Standard 6 – Literature and Culture

Students read and recognize literature as a record and expression of cultural heritage.

❑ Read, respond to, and discuss a variety of literature (for example: folk tales, legends, myths, fiction, rhymes and poems, nonfiction, and content-area reading).

Directions: For questions 1–4 read the poem. Then darken the circle for the correct answer to each question.

Moveable Art

Cumulus patches in cerulean blue
Curious patterns happen
Amazing animals
bizarre bird beaks
Clipper ships
and a barque sail by
Faces of laughing children
shift, move, change

Painted by the wind
brushstrokes rearranged
Bits and pieces
float in and out
Depart

Beatrice G. Davis

1. Why does the poet call her poem "Moveable Art"?
   Ⓐ The clouds move through the sky.
   Ⓑ The paintings can be changed.
   Ⓒ Children laugh and change.
   Ⓓ There are bizarre bird beaks.

2. From this poem you can tell that a <u>barque</u> is a kind of _____.
   Ⓐ tree
   Ⓑ cloud
   Ⓒ boat
   Ⓓ face

3. What causes the brushstrokes to be rearranged?
   Ⓐ amazing animals
   Ⓑ the wind
   Ⓒ bits and pieces
   Ⓓ clipper ships

4. What makes curious patterns happen?
   Ⓐ cumulus patches
   Ⓑ cerulean blue
   Ⓒ the movement of the clouds
   Ⓓ bizarre birds

Answers:
1. A, 2. C, 3. B, 4. C

MATH

Standard 1 – Number Sense

Students develop number sense, use numbers and number relationships in problem-solving situations, and communicate the reasoning used in solving these problems.

❑ Read, write, order, and compare whole numbers, integers, unit fractions (e.g. $\frac{1}{4}, \frac{1}{5}$) with unlike denominators, and decimals to hundredths as they relate to money.

Directions: For questions 1–6 darken the circle for the correct answer.

---

1. Which of these number sentences is true?
   Ⓐ 4,156 > 4,257
   Ⓑ 8,651 = 8000 + 600 + 15
   Ⓒ 375 < 379
   Ⓓ 1,332 > 1,432

2. Which number is the greatest?
   Ⓐ 9,929
   Ⓑ 9,990
   Ⓒ 9,959
   Ⓓ 9,995

3. Which number is less than 968 and greater than 961?
   Ⓐ 970
   Ⓑ 960
   Ⓒ 969
   Ⓓ 964

4. Nina used $\frac{2}{3}$ cup of sugar in her apple muffins. Laurel used $\frac{5}{8}$ cup sugar in her apple muffins. How much more sugar did Nina use?
   Ⓐ $\frac{3}{8}$
   Ⓑ $\frac{1}{3}$
   Ⓒ $\frac{1}{24}$
   Ⓓ $\frac{1}{4}$

5. Which decimal number has a 4 in the tens place, a 3 in the ones place, and a 5 in the hundredths place?
   Ⓐ 43.05
   Ⓑ 534.00
   Ⓒ 53.40
   Ⓓ 4.305

6. Which number sentence shows the correct placement of the < or > sign?
   Ⓐ 415 > 515
   Ⓑ 749 < 721
   Ⓒ 5 < 1
   Ⓓ 45 > 41

Answers:
1. C, **2.** D, **3.** D, **4.** C, **5.** A, **6.** D

Standard 2 –Patterns and Algebra

Students use algebraic methods to explore, model, and describe patterns and functions involving numbers, shapes, data, and graphs in problem-solving situations and communicate the reasoning used in solving these problems.

❑ Use tables, graphs, open sentences ($n + 5 = 12$), and relational diagrams to describe patterns and other relationships (bar, circle, and broken line graphs).

Directions: Use this graph to answer questions 1 and 2.

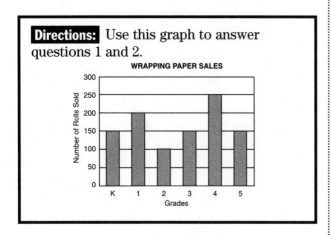

1. How many rolls of wrapping paper did the students in grade 3 sell?
   Ⓐ 100 rolls
   Ⓑ 150 rolls
   Ⓒ 200 rolls
   Ⓓ 250 rolls

2. How many rolls were sold by grades 2, 3, and 4 altogether?
   Ⓐ 400 rolls
   Ⓑ 650 rolls
   Ⓒ 300 rolls
   Ⓓ 500 rolls

Standard 3 –Statistics and Probability

Students use data collection and analysis, statistics, and probability in problem-solving situations and communicate the reasoning used in solving these problems.

❑ Generate, analyze, and make predictions based on data (with one variable) obtained from surveys and chance devices (for example: spinners and dice).

Directions: For questions 3–4 darken the circle for the correct answer.

3. On which shape will the arrow stop the least number of times?
   Ⓐ pentagon
   Ⓑ square
   Ⓒ circle
   Ⓓ triangle

4. Which animal will the spinner land on the most number of times?
   Ⓐ Panther
   Ⓑ Dolphin
   Ⓒ Monkey
   Ⓓ Otter

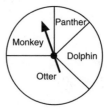

Answers:
1. B, 2. D, 3. C, 4. D

Standard 4 –Geometry

Students use geometric concepts, properties, and relationships in problem-solving situations and communicate the reasoning used in solving these problems.

❑ Identify, classify, describe, and compare models of the two- and three-dimensional geometric figures previously identified.

❑ Use a grid to recreate two-dimensional figures of a given shape, area, and perimeter (circle, triangle, square, or rectangle) and determine its area and perimeter.

Directions: For questions 1–6 darken the circle for the correct answer.

1. What is the perimeter of this chalkboard if it is expressed in feet?

   Ⓐ 12 feet
   Ⓑ 8 feet
   Ⓒ 20 feet
   Ⓓ 10 feet

2. What is the name of this figure?

   Ⓐ pentagon
   Ⓑ triangle
   Ⓒ parallelogram
   Ⓓ square

3. Which of these lines are intersecting?

   Ⓐ   Ⓑ   Ⓒ   Ⓓ

4. How many angles does this figure have?

   Ⓐ 5 angles
   Ⓑ 8 angles
   Ⓒ 4 angles
   Ⓓ 6 angles

5. Which of these is a chord?

   Ⓐ AC
   Ⓑ CB
   Ⓒ AB
   Ⓓ CD

6. What is the area of the shaded area in square units?

   Ⓐ 20
   Ⓑ 35
   Ⓒ 45
   Ⓓ 30

   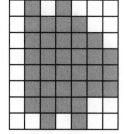

Answers:
1. A, **2.** C, **3.** A, **4.** D, **5.** C, **6.** B

Standard 5 –Measurement

Students use a variety of tools and techniques to measure, apply the results in problem-solving situations, and communicate the reasoning used in solving these problems.

❑ Estimate and measure length (yards and meters), area, capacity (milliliters and liters), weight (gram and kilogram), time (minute intervals), and temperature (Fahrenheit) using standard units of measurement with an understanding of the results.

Directions: For questions 1–6 darken the circle for the correct answer.

1. How many inches are there between point B and point A?

   Ⓐ 1 $\frac{1}{2}$ inches

   Ⓑ 3 inches

   Ⓒ 1 inch

   Ⓓ 2 $\frac{1}{2}$ inches

2. How many centimeters are there between point J and point K?

   Ⓐ 1 $\frac{1}{2}$

   Ⓑ 3

   Ⓒ 3 $\frac{1}{2}$

   Ⓓ 5

   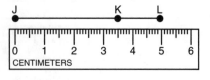

3. Which of these clocks shows 11:45?

   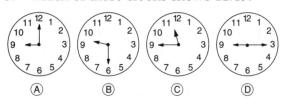

   Ⓐ   Ⓑ   Ⓒ   Ⓓ

4. What time is four hours after 3:15 p.m.?

   Ⓐ 7:00 P.M.

   Ⓑ 1:15 P.M.

   Ⓒ 7:15 P.M.

   Ⓓ 6:45 P.M.

5. What is the temperature on this thermometer?

   Ⓐ 68°

   Ⓑ 72°

   Ⓒ 70°

   Ⓓ 69°

   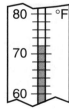

6. How many inches long is rod C?

   Ⓐ 4 $\frac{1}{2}$ inches

   Ⓑ 2 inches

   Ⓒ 1 $\frac{1}{2}$ inches

   Ⓓ 3 $\frac{1}{2}$ inches

   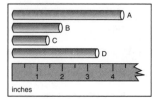

Answers:
1. A, **2.** C, **3.** C, **4.** C, **5.** B **6.** C

Standard 6 –Computation

Students link concepts and procedures as they develop and use computational techniques, including estimation, mental arithmetic, paper and pencil, calculators, and computers in problem-solving situations and communicate the reasoning used in solving these problems.

❑ Develop procedures for computing and estimating with whole numbers using the four basic arithmetic operations.

Directions: For questions 1–6 darken the circle of the correct answer.

1. Chelsea needs 24 feet of lace for her costume. The lace is sold by the yard. How many yards of lace will she need?

   Ⓐ 9 yards

   Ⓑ 10 yards

   Ⓒ 8 yards

   Ⓓ 6 yards

2. There are thirty felt-tip pens to be shared equally among ten children. How many pens can each child have? Choose the correct operation.

   Ⓐ +

   Ⓑ −

   Ⓒ ×

   Ⓓ ÷

3. Apple pies at the harvest festival were cut into 5 equal portions. There were 45 portions in all. Which number sentence should you use to find out how many pies were served?

   Ⓐ $45 + 5 = ?$

   Ⓑ $45 \div 5 = ?$

   Ⓒ $45 \times 5 = ?$

   Ⓓ $45 - 5 = ?$

4. A group of 79 fourth-grade students and 98 third-grade students are going on a field trip. The cafeteria is supplying bag lunches for all the students. They are also supplying small packages of trail mix for a snack. About how many packages of trail mix will they need?

   Ⓐ 210 packages

   Ⓑ 80 packages

   Ⓒ 100 packages

   Ⓓ 180 packages

5. Estimate the sum of 19, 21, and 29.

   Ⓐ 50

   Ⓑ 40

   Ⓒ 60

   Ⓓ 70

6. Gail has 1 quarter, 2 nickels, and 7 pennies. How much more money does she need to buy a $.79 treat?

   Ⓐ $0.37

   Ⓑ $0.17

   Ⓒ $0.27

   Ⓓ $0.35

Answers:
1. C, **2.** D, **3.** B, **4.** D, **5.** D, **6.** A

SCIENCE

Standard 1 –Physical Science

Students understand common properties, forms, and changes in matter and energy (with a focus on physics and chemistry).

❑ Examine, describe, classify, and compare tangible objects in terms of common physical properties (for example: state of matter, size, shape, texture, flexibility, color).

Directions: For questions 1-5 darken the circle for the correct answer.

1. Matter keeps its own shape when it is in the form of
   Ⓐ a solid.
   Ⓑ a liquid.
   Ⓒ a gas.
   Ⓓ all of the above.

2. All of the following are the same form of matter except
   Ⓐ milk.
   Ⓑ lemon juice.
   Ⓒ oil.
   Ⓓ steam.

3. The three states of matter are
   Ⓐ nitrogen, oxygen, carbon dioxide.
   Ⓑ solids, liquids, gases.
   Ⓒ evaporation, condensation, precipitation.
   Ⓓ rocks, sand, soil.

4. Moving gas from a jar to a balloon would change
   Ⓐ the shape of the gas.
   Ⓑ the gas to liquid.
   Ⓒ the color of the gas.
   Ⓓ nothing.

5. Cardboard is an ___ material.
   Ⓐ oily.
   Ⓑ average.
   Ⓒ opaque.
   Ⓓ empty.

Answers:
1. A, **2.** D, **3.** B, **4.** A, **5.** C

Standard 2 –Life Science

Students understand the characteristics and structure of living things, the processes of life, and how living things interact with each other and their environment (with a focus on biology, anatomy, physiology, botany, zoology, ecology).

❑ Identify digestive, respiratory, and circulatory systems of the human body.

Directions: For questions 1-5 darken the circle for the correct answer.

1. This body system is used for breathing.
   Ⓐ digestive
   Ⓑ respiratory
   Ⓒ skeletal
   Ⓓ circulatory

2. Food is changed to useful materials in the ___ system.
   Ⓐ digestive
   Ⓑ respiratory
   Ⓒ skeletal
   Ⓓ circulatory

3. The heart is part of the ___ system.
   Ⓐ digestive
   Ⓑ respiratory
   Ⓒ skeletal
   Ⓓ circulatory

4. The lungs are part of the ___ system.
   Ⓐ digestive
   Ⓑ respiratory
   Ⓒ skeletal
   Ⓓ circulatory

5. The stomach is part of the ___ system.
   Ⓐ digestive
   Ⓑ respiratory
   Ⓒ skeletal
   Ⓓ circulatory

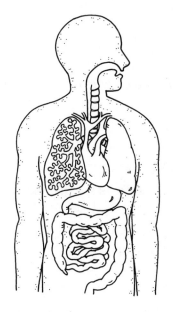

Answers:
1. B, 2. A, 3. D, 4. B, 5. A

Standard 3 –Earth and Space Science

Students understand the processes and interactions of Earth's systems and the structure and dynamics of Earth and other objects in space (with a focus on geology, meteorology, astronomy, oceanography).

❑ Describe natural processes that change Earth's surface (weathering, erosion, mountain building, volcanic activity).

Directions: For questions 1-5 darken the circle for the correct answer.

1. What changes in a rock during physical weathering?
   Ⓐ color
   Ⓑ size and shape
   Ⓒ the inside of the rock
   Ⓓ nothing

2. Erosion occurs when
   Ⓐ soil is added to the ground.
   Ⓑ dams are built.
   Ⓒ rocks and soil are carried away by wind and water.
   Ⓓ grass and trees are planted.

3. Material carried by rivers to the ocean is called
   Ⓐ rust.
   Ⓑ deltas.
   Ⓒ sediment.
   Ⓓ carbon dioxide.

4. An earthquake is
   Ⓐ an opening in the Earth's crust through which lava escapes.
   Ⓑ a sudden movement in the Earth's crust.
   Ⓒ never the cause of much damage.
   Ⓓ a kind of chemical weathering.

5. A machine that measures earthquakes is a
   Ⓐ seismograph.
   Ⓑ phonograph.
   Ⓒ vulcanizer.
   Ⓓ telescope.

Answers:
1. B, 2. C, 3. C, 4. B, 5. A

FIFTH GRADE

Language Arts
Math
Science

PARENTS' GUIDE TO TESTING

LANGUAGE ARTS

Standard 1 – Reading

Students read and understand a variety of materials.

❑ Use comprehension strategies: preview, predict and confirm, compare and contrast.

Directions: For questions 1–4 read the selection. Then darken the circle for the correct answer to each question.

Jove, a Greek god, had many sons. He was thought of as being cheerful and hearty. Today when we describe someone as being cheerful, we say that person is very *jovial*. Jove also had a sister named Ceres. She was the goddess of agriculture. The word *cereal* comes from her name.

Mars is the name of a planet and of a famous son of the Greek god Jove. Mars is the god of war, so when we speak of military things, we often use the word *martial*. When we talk about people who might live on the planet Mars, we call them *Martians*. The month of March is named for Mars.

January is named for Janus, another son of Jove. Janus had two faces, one in front, looking ahead, and one in back, looking to the past. Perhaps the month of January was named for Janus because it comes after the old year and at the beginning of the new year.

1. What is the main idea of this selection?
   Ⓐ to tell about Jove and his sons
   Ⓑ to tell about planets that are named for Greek gods
   Ⓒ to tell how some words became part of our language
   Ⓓ to teach us more about Greek mythology

2. Why does the author compare the god Janus to the month of January?
   Ⓐ January is a cold month.
   Ⓑ January faces the old and the new.
   Ⓒ Janus was a good son.
   Ⓓ Janus was the brother of Mars.

3. Which of these could be a title for this article?
   Ⓐ Words We Get from Greek Mythology
   Ⓑ Jove and His Sons
   Ⓒ Greek Gods and Their Planets
   Ⓓ The Martians Are Coming

4. If someone you know likes to have fun, you might say that person is most like _____.
   Ⓐ Janus
   Ⓑ Ceres
   Ⓒ Mars
   Ⓓ Jove

Answers:
1. C, 2. B, 3. A, 4. D

Standard 2 – Writing and Speaking

Students write and speak for a variety of purposes and audiences.

❏ Vary word choices by using devices such as synonyms and antonyms, descriptive language, figures of speech (for example: simile and metaphor).

> **Directions:** For questions 1–2 darken the circle for the word or group of words that means the *same* or *almost the same* as the underlined word.

1. A <u>sturdy</u> rope
   - Ⓐ strong
   - Ⓑ long
   - Ⓒ thin
   - Ⓓ twisted

2. <u>Ancient</u> equipment
   - Ⓐ used
   - Ⓑ discarded
   - Ⓒ obsolete
   - Ⓓ useful

> **Directions:** For questions 3–4 darken the circle for the word that means the *opposite* of the underlined word.

3. A <u>smooth</u> road
   - Ⓐ paved
   - Ⓑ narrow
   - Ⓒ curvy
   - Ⓓ rough

4. A <u>murky</u> sky
   - Ⓐ clear
   - Ⓑ dark
   - Ⓒ dismal
   - Ⓓ cloudy

Standard 3 – Language Structure

Students write and speak using conventional grammar, usage, sentence structure, punctuation, capitalization, and spelling.

❏ Use appropriate end punctuation in sentences.

❏ Correctly punctuate singular possessives.

> **Directions:** For questions 5–6 darken the circle for the sentence that shows correct capitalization and punctuation.

5. Ⓐ One boys' bike was missing.
   - Ⓑ Take off your hat inside the house please.
   - Ⓒ Don't touch that poisonous spider!
   - Ⓓ Sammi asked where is my mom?

6. Ⓐ I like salt pepper and mustard on hot dogs.
   - Ⓑ On Friday, April 5, we'll have a concert.
   - Ⓒ Let me introduce you to Tony?
   - Ⓓ Lucys report was about fossils.

> **Answers:**
> **1.** A, **2.** C, **3.** D, **4.** A, **5.** C, **6.** B

Standard 4 –Thinking and Viewing

Students apply thinking skills to their reading, writing, speaking, listening, and viewing.

❑ Draw conclusions.

Directions: For questions 1–3 read the selection. Then darken the circle for the correct answer to each question.

A huge sunken tube tunnel is being built as part of a bridge-tunnel between Sweden and Denmark. It will be Sweden's first direct road and rail link to the rest of Europe.

When construction workers came to the thirteenth of twenty parts they had to install, they numbered it 12A. Changing the number didn't do any good. Part 12A sank accidentally in early August. The accident caused a two-month delay in the project.

Project officials still expect the bridge-tunnel to open in 2000. At that time the Danish capital of Copenhagen will be connected to the Swedish port city of Malmö. Instead of taking a ferry from Sweden to Denmark, people will be able to drive from one country to another!

1. Why did the workers change the number on the thirteenth part?
   Ⓐ They thought there would be more than twenty parts.
   Ⓑ They were superstitious.
   Ⓒ They thought it would sink.
   Ⓓ They were afraid of a two-month delay.

2. How will people travel between Denmark and Sweden until the bridge-tunnel is finished?
   Ⓐ by car
   Ⓑ by train
   Ⓒ by ferry
   Ⓓ by bus

3. Why is this bridge-tunnel important to the people of Sweden?
   Ⓐ They're tired of waiting for ferries.
   Ⓑ They like shopping in the capital.
   Ⓒ It has a sunken tube.
   Ⓓ It will connect them to the rest of Europe.

Answers:
1. B, 2. C, 3. D

Standard 5 –Research

Students read to locate, select, and make use of relevant information from a variety of media, reference, and technological sources.

❏ Locate specific information using computer card catalog, table of contents in a book, and index in a book.

Directions: Use the Table of Contents to answer questions 1–5. Darken the circle for the correct answer to each question.

Contents

1. From the table of contents, you can guess that this book is about what?
   Ⓐ getting a job
   Ⓑ doing well in school
   Ⓒ getting along with others
   Ⓓ writing good book reports

2. Which chapter tells about using your memory?
   Ⓐ Chapter 1
   Ⓑ Chapter 6
   Ⓒ Chapter 5
   Ⓓ Chapter 3

3. How many pages teach you ways to tackle your homework?
   Ⓐ 14 pages
   Ⓑ 15 pages
   Ⓒ 18 pages
   Ⓓ 10 pages

4. Which chapter teaches you how to take notes?
   Ⓐ Chapter 6
   Ⓑ Chapter 3
   Ⓒ Chapter 2
   Ⓓ Chapter 1

5. On what page does the chapter on taking tests begin?
   Ⓐ page 77
   Ⓑ page 31
   Ⓒ page 1
   Ⓓ page 17

Answers:
1. B, **2.** C, **3.** A, **4.** D, **5.** A

Standard 6 – Literature and Culture

Students read and recognize literature as a record and expression of cultural heritage.

❑ Identify setting, plot, and main character in a story or poem.

Directions: For questions 1–3 read the poem. Then darken the circle for the correct answer to each question.

Curtain Time

Standing silently among the others
through months of heat, wind, rain,
    and Sun
Your sameness a backdrop
your greenness, soothing,
calming.
Distracted
audiences pass by
immersed in private thoughts

Presently you erupt into color—
    rust, orange, gold,
no longer one of many.
Stepping onto center stage
you bask in your moment
of glory...then
fade into the scenery
and wait silently with the others.

Beatrice G. Davis

1. What season of the year is this poem about?
  Ⓐ winter
  Ⓑ spring
  Ⓒ summer
  Ⓓ fall

2. To whom is the poet speaking?
  Ⓐ audiences
  Ⓑ a tree
  Ⓒ heat
  Ⓓ rain

3. Which words tell you that the poet thinks of this scene as a stage set?
  Ⓐ wait silently with the others
  Ⓑ no longer one of many
  Ⓒ fade into the scenery
  Ⓓ presently you erupt

Answers:
1. D, **2.** B, **3.** C

MATH

Standard 1 – Number Sense

Students develop number sense, use numbers and number relationships in problem-solving situations, and communicate the reasoning used in solving these problems.

❑ Identify the relationships among the concepts of fractions, decimal numbers, and division.

Directions: For questions 1–6 darken the circle for the correct answer.

---

1. Which fraction shows the ratio of 17 to 15?
   - Ⓐ $\frac{17}{15}$
   - Ⓑ $\frac{15}{17}$
   - Ⓒ $1\frac{2}{15}$
   - Ⓓ $\frac{17}{25}$

2. Which pair of ratios is equal?
   - Ⓐ $\frac{27}{54}$, $\frac{9}{18}$
   - Ⓑ $\frac{12}{5}$, $\frac{4}{25}$
   - Ⓒ $\frac{6}{12}$, $\frac{1}{12}$
   - Ⓓ $\frac{7}{4}$, $\frac{35}{8}$

3. Change 2% to a decimal.
   - Ⓐ 0.02
   - Ⓑ 2.0
   - Ⓒ 0.2
   - Ⓓ 20.00

4. Change $\frac{9}{25}$ to a percent.
   - Ⓐ 25%
   - Ⓑ 90%
   - Ⓒ 36%
   - Ⓓ 10%

5. If sales tax is 5%, what is the amount of tax on items that cost $1.78 and $2.36?
   - Ⓐ 32¢
   - Ⓑ 21¢
   - Ⓒ 25¢
   - Ⓓ 18¢

6. Marcella's mother baked muffins and breads for the holiday. She used $1\frac{1}{2}$ pounds of nuts for both recipes. If she used $\frac{3}{4}$ pound of nuts for the muffins, how much did she use for the breads?
   - Ⓐ 1 pound
   - Ⓑ $\frac{1}{2}$ pound
   - Ⓒ $\frac{1}{4}$ pound
   - Ⓓ $\frac{3}{4}$ pound

Answers:
1. A, **2.** A, **3.** A, **4.** C, **5.** B, **6.** D

© Steck-Vaughn Company

Standard 2 – Patterns and Algebra

Students use algebraic methods to explore, model, and describe patterns and functions involving numbers, shapes, data, and graphs in problem-solving situations and communicate the reasoning used in solving these problems.

❑ Recognize linear relationships (for example: if one candy bar costs $.50, then two candy bars cost $1.00).

> **Directions:** For questions 1–2 darken the circle for the correct answer.

1. Tanya bought 3 boxes of plant food for her African violets. Each box cost $0.75. How much did the plant food cost altogether?
   - Ⓐ $2.25
   - Ⓑ $2.10
   - Ⓒ $1.75
   - Ⓓ $1.50

2. Ramona and her roommate signed a three-year lease for an apartment. Each of them will pay $220 a month for rent. How much money will Ramona have spent for rent by the time the lease is over?
   - Ⓐ $7,920.00
   - Ⓑ $790.20
   - Ⓒ $8,290.00
   - Ⓓ $79,200.00

Standard 3 – Statistics and Probability

Students use data collection and analysis, statistics, and probability in problem-solving situations and communicate the reasoning used in solving these problems.

❑ Make predictions and compare results using experimental probability of one variable.

> **Directions:** Answer questions 3–4 about these cards. Darken the circle for the correct answer.

3. What is the probability of choosing a card with the letter A?
   - Ⓐ $\frac{8}{10}$
   - Ⓑ $\frac{1}{5}$
   - Ⓒ $\frac{2}{5}$
   - Ⓓ $\frac{4}{5}$

4. What is the probability of choosing a card with the letter C?
   - Ⓐ $\frac{9}{10}$
   - Ⓑ $\frac{7}{10}$
   - Ⓒ $\frac{3}{10}$
   - Ⓓ $\frac{1}{10}$

> **Answers:**
> 1. A, 2. A, 3. B, 4. D

Standard 4 –Geometry

Students use geometric concepts, properties, and relationships in problem-solving situations and communicate the reasoning used in solving these problems.

❏ Know properties and vocabulary of quadrilaterals, squares, rectangles, parallelograms, circles, and triangles.

Directions: For questions 1–6 darken the circle for the correct answer. Darken the circle for *Not given* if the correct answer is *not* given.

1. Which of these figures shows a line of symmetry?

   A　　**B**　　**C**　　**D**

   Ⓐ A
   Ⓑ B
   Ⓒ C
   Ⓓ Not given

2. Which numbers are on triangles in this figure?
   Ⓐ 3, 4, 2
   Ⓑ 2, 1, 5
   Ⓒ 4, 1, 3
   Ⓓ Not given

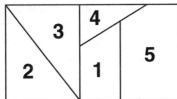

3. Which of these is a radius?
   Ⓐ AB
   Ⓑ CD
   Ⓒ BD
   Ⓓ Not given

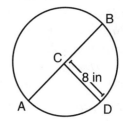

4. Which of these is a chord?
   Ⓐ AX
   Ⓑ AB
   Ⓒ BX
   Ⓓ Not given

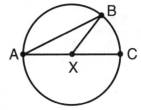

5. What is the name of this figure?
   Ⓐ rectangle
   Ⓑ trapezoid
   Ⓒ parallelogram
   Ⓓ Not given

6. How are these figures alike?

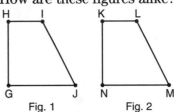

   Fig. 1　　Fig. 2

   Ⓐ They are perpendicular.
   Ⓑ They are congruent.
   Ⓒ They are intersecting.
   Ⓓ Not given

Answers:
1. B, **2.** A, **3.** B, **4.** B, **5.** C, **6.** B

Standard 5 – Measurement

Students use a variety of tools and techniques to measure, apply the results in problem-solving situations, and communicate the reasoning used in solving these problems.

❑ Use area and perimeter formulas to calculate the area and perimeters of squares, rectangles, and other figures.

Directions: For questions 1–6 darken the circle for the correct answer. Darken the circle for *Not given* if the correct answer is *not* given.

1. What is the perimeter of this figure?
   Ⓐ 24 cm
   Ⓑ 12 cm
   Ⓒ 36 cm
   Ⓓ Not given

   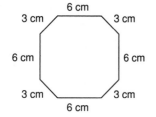

2. What is the perimeter of this figure?
   Ⓐ 36 inches
   Ⓑ 24 inches
   Ⓒ 18 inches
   Ⓓ Not given

3. What is the area of this rectangle?

   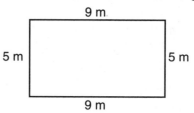

   Ⓐ 28 square meters
   Ⓑ 18 square meters
   Ⓒ 45 square meters
   Ⓓ Not given

4. How much would it cost to carpet a room that is 18 feet long and 15 feet wide if the carpet costs $18.50 a square yard?
   What strategy should you use to solve this problem?
   Ⓐ Guess and check
   Ⓑ Choose the operation
   Ⓒ Use a multi-step plan
   Ⓓ Make a graph

5. Buddy's room is 12 feet long and 9 feet wide. If Buddy's parents put down a new floor in his room, how many square feet of flooring will they need?
   Ⓐ 21 square feet
   Ⓑ 108 square feet
   Ⓒ 12 square feet
   Ⓓ 120 square feet

6. The Anderson family is planning to put a fence around their garden. The garden is 82 feet long and 36 feet wide. How much fencing will they need to go around the perimeter of the garden?
   Ⓐ 164 feet
   Ⓑ 72 feet
   Ⓒ 118 feet
   Ⓓ 236 feet

Answers:
1. C, **2.** B, **3.** C, **4.** C, **5.** B, **6.** D

Standard 6 –Computation

Students link concepts and procedures as they develop and use computational techniques, including estimation, mental arithmetic, paper and pencil, calculators, and computers, in problem-solving situations and communicate the reasoning used in solving these problems.

❑ Select and use appropriate methods for computing with whole numbers and commonly used fractions, decimals, and percents in problem-solving situations from among mental arithmetic, estimations, pencil-and-paper algorithms, and calculator or other mechanical methods in the four basic arithmetic operations.

Directions: For questions 1–6 darken the circle for the correct answer.

1. The Allenwood School has 408 fiction books in the library. There are 219 biographies in the library. What operation should you use to find how many more fiction books than biography books the library has?

   Ⓐ addition

   Ⓑ subtraction

   Ⓒ multiplication

   Ⓓ division

2. A recipe calls for $2\frac{1}{4}$ cups of flour. The recipe makes eight servings. How many cups of flour will be needed to make 24 servings?
   What strategy should you use to solve this problem?

   Ⓐ Work backwards

   Ⓑ Use a multi-step plan

   Ⓒ Guess and check

   Ⓓ Make a pattern

3. If a year has 365 days and a day has 24 hours, how many hours are there in a year?

   Ⓐ 7,860 hours

   Ⓑ 6,780 hours

   Ⓒ 8,670 hours

   Ⓓ 8,760 hours

4. Mimi and her friend are planning to visit Washington, D.C., for a three-day weekend. They estimate that they will each spend about $90.00 a day. About how much money will Mimi and her friend need altogether for the weekend?

   Ⓐ $540

   Ⓑ $270

   Ⓒ $90

   Ⓓ $180

5. Rudy bought a 36-exposure roll of film for $4.80. It cost him $6 to have the film developed. What was the average cost per picture?

   Ⓐ $6

   Ⓑ 30¢

   Ⓒ 68¢

   Ⓓ 80¢

6. Ricky had $20.00 when he went to the mall last Saturday. He bought a gift for $6.95 and spent $4.89 on lunch. How much money did he still have when he went home?

   Ⓐ $7.00

   Ⓑ $6.18

   Ⓒ $5.29

   Ⓓ $8.16

Answers:
1. B, **2.** B, **3.** D, **4.** A, **5.** B, **6.** D

SCIENCE

Standard 1 –Physical Science

Students understand common properties, forms, and changes in matter and energy (with a focus on physics and chemistry).

❏ Predict outcomes by changing variables.

❏ Design and conduct experiments using simple machines (for example: pendulums, catapults, pulleys, levers).

❏ Measure force, distance, and work involved using levers and pulleys.

❏ Identify and classify factors causing change within a system.

Directions: For questions 1–5 darken the circle for the correct answer.

---

1. Cutting paper is an example of a
   Ⓐ chemical change.
   Ⓑ electrical change.
   Ⓒ physical change.
   Ⓓ gravitational change.

2. Water can change into a gas through
   Ⓐ condensation.
   Ⓑ evaporation.
   Ⓒ precipitation.
   Ⓓ acceleration.

3. Hydrogen and oxygen make
   Ⓐ carbon dioxide.
   Ⓑ salt.
   Ⓒ mercuric oxide.
   Ⓓ water.

4. An example of a chemical reaction is
   Ⓐ a burning fire.
   Ⓑ a reaction between vinegar and baking soda.
   Ⓒ rusting iron.
   Ⓓ all of the above.

5. When two substances go through a chemical change,
   Ⓐ they always turn into gases.
   Ⓑ their physical properties remain the same.
   Ⓒ their molecules remain the same.
   Ⓓ they form a new substance with different properties.

Answers:
1. C, 2. B, 3. D, 4. D, 5. D

Standard 2 –Life Science

Students understand the characteristics and structure of living things, the processes of life, and how living things interact with each other and their environment (with a focus on biology, anatomy, physiology, botany, zoology, ecology).

❑ Based on attributes, place living organisms into groups based on similarities.

❑ Identify living and nonliving components of an ecosystem when given an example of one.

❑ Identify the characteristics of healthy, functioning ecosystems.

❑ Explain the interaction and interdependence of nonliving and living components within ecosystems.

Directions: For questions 1-5 darken the circle for the correct answer.

1. Animals that live part of their lives in water and part on land are called
   Ⓐ mammals.
   Ⓑ insects.
   Ⓒ amphibians.
   Ⓓ reptiles.

2. Animals with backbones are called
   Ⓐ vertebrates.
   Ⓑ invertebrates.
   Ⓒ arthropods.
   Ⓓ frogs.

3. Animals with hair or fur are called
   Ⓐ birds.
   Ⓑ mammals.
   Ⓒ reptiles.
   Ⓓ cold-blooded.

4. Plants that reproduce by seeds in cones are called
   Ⓐ warm-blooded.
   Ⓑ invertebrates.
   Ⓒ angiosperms.
   Ⓓ arthropods.

5. Insects are the largest part of a group of animals called
   Ⓐ arthropods.
   Ⓑ angiosperms.
   Ⓒ amphibians.
   Ⓓ reptiles.

Answers:
1. C, 2. A, 3. B, 4. C, 5. A

Standard 3 – Earth and Space Science

Students understand the processes and interactions of Earth's systems and the structure and dynamics of Earth and other objects in space (with a focus on geology, meteorology, astronomy, oceanography).

❑ Explain the H_2O cycle and identify sources of fresh and salt H_2O.

❑ Describe differences in salt and fresh water (salinity).

❑ Explore uses of water in production of energy.

Directions: For questions 1-5 darken the circle for the correct answer.

---

1. The water cycle is
   Ⓐ the movement of water between the air and the ground.
   Ⓑ a form of transportation.
   Ⓒ a weather symbol.
   Ⓓ an air mass.

2. The three steps of the water cycle are
   Ⓐ igneous, sedimentary, and metamorphic.
   Ⓑ troposphere, stratosphere, and ionosphere.
   Ⓒ evaporation, condensation, and precipitation.
   Ⓓ rain, snow, and fog.

3. Humidity is the amount of
   Ⓐ oxygen in the air.
   Ⓑ water vapor in the air.
   Ⓒ dust in the air.
   Ⓓ rain that falls.

4. Most of the water in the oceans is
   Ⓐ fifty miles deep.
   Ⓑ fresh water.
   Ⓒ magnetic.
   Ⓓ salt water.

5. Clouds, rain, and wind are all part of the Earth's
   Ⓐ core.
   Ⓑ ionosphere.
   Ⓒ weather.
   Ⓓ gravity.

Answers:
1. A, **2.** C, **3.** B, **4.** D, **5.** C

SIXTH GRADE

Language Arts
Math
Science

PARENTS' GUIDE TO TESTING

SIXTH GRADE

 # LANGUAGE ARTS

Standard 1 –Reading

Students read and understand a variety of materials.

❑ Use word parts (roots, prefixes, suffixes) to increase vocabulary.

> **Directions:** For questions 1–6 darken the circle for the word or words that give the best meaning of the underlined prefix or suffix.

1. <u>dis</u>locate   <u>dis</u>able
   - Ⓐ not
   - Ⓑ deprive
   - Ⓒ allow
   - Ⓓ change

2. <u>bi</u>sect   <u>bi</u>annual
   - Ⓐ one time
   - Ⓑ divide equally
   - Ⓒ more than one
   - Ⓓ not entirely

3. hero<u>ic</u>   titan<u>ic</u>
   - Ⓐ together
   - Ⓑ ever
   - Ⓒ like
   - Ⓓ from

4. <u>il</u>logical   <u>il</u>legal
   - Ⓐ not
   - Ⓑ always
   - Ⓒ again
   - Ⓓ full of

5. fear<u>less</u>   joy<u>less</u>
   - Ⓐ together
   - Ⓑ full of
   - Ⓒ without
   - Ⓓ into

6. just<u>ly</u>   harsh<u>ly</u>
   - Ⓐ in a certain way
   - Ⓑ afterward
   - Ⓒ in a while
   - Ⓓ in a positive way

> **Answers:**
> **1.** A, **2.** B, **3.** C, **4.** A, **5.** C, **6.** A

Standard 2 –Writing and Speaking

Students write and speak for a variety of purposes and audiences.

❑ Edit and revise with guidance.

Directions: For questions 1–5 read the selection. Then darken the circle for the correct answer to each question.

Running is a very popular sport. Early in the morning you can see people running in my city. You can see people running in the country. Next week I'm getting new running shoes. Everyone in my family likes to run. My father likes to run before work each morning. My mother and sister run before dinner I like to run with my dog every Saturday morning! We run to the city park. I meet my friends at the city park.

1. Which is the topic sentence?
   Ⓐ Sentence 5
   Ⓑ Sentence 1
   Ⓒ Sentence 4
   Ⓓ Sentence 2

2. Which sentence doesn't belong in the paragraph?
   Ⓐ Sentence 6
   Ⓑ Sentence 3
   Ⓒ Sentence 1
   Ⓓ Sentence 7

3. Which is a run-on sentence?
   Ⓐ Sentence 7
   Ⓑ Sentence 5
   Ⓒ Sentence 8
   Ⓓ Sentence 3

4. Which sentences could be combined?
   Ⓐ Sentences 1 and 2
   Ⓑ Sentences 8 and 9
   Ⓒ Sentences 7 and 8
   Ⓓ Sentences 3 and 4

5. Which sentence has incorrect punctuation?
   Ⓐ Sentence 1
   Ⓑ Sentence 3
   Ⓒ Sentence 7
   Ⓓ Sentence 4

Answers:
1. B, **2.** B, **3.** A, **4.** B, **5.** C

Standard 3 – Language Structure

Students write and speak using conventional grammar, usage, sentence structure, punctuation, capitalization, and spelling.

❑ Correctly spell commonly used words.

Directions: For questions 1–3 darken the circle for the word that is spelled correctly.

1. You need to be _____ when you train a dog.
   Ⓐ pashent
   Ⓑ patient
   Ⓒ pashient
   Ⓓ paitent

2. Did you get your _____ slip signed?
   Ⓐ permission
   Ⓑ permition
   Ⓒ permision
   Ⓓ pirmission

3. How _____ do you visit the dentist?
   Ⓐ offen
   Ⓑ often
   Ⓒ oftin
   Ⓓ offin

Standard 4 – Thinking and Viewing

Students apply thinking skills to their reading, writing, speaking, listening, and viewing.

❑ Practice identifying cause and effect.

Directions: For questions 4–5 read the selection. Then darken the circle for the correct answer to each question.

If the Earth's temperature heats up as mainstream scientists predict it will over the next century, the average level of the world's oceans could rise. Scientists think that the level could rise as much as a foot and a half by the year 2100, and somewhat more after that. Glaciers would partly melt into the sea, making the water expand. Low-lying coastal areas would surely be inundated.

4. What could happen if Earth's temperature rises?
   Ⓐ Air-conditioning would cost more.
   Ⓑ Heaters might become obsolete.
   Ⓒ The level of the oceans could rise.
   Ⓓ More icebergs might form.

5. What could happen if the level of Earth's oceans rises?
   Ⓐ Surfing would improve.
   Ⓑ Low-lying areas might be flooded.
   Ⓒ Glaciers could get larger.
   Ⓓ More ships might sink.

Answers:
1. B, 2. A, 3. B, 4. C, 5. B

Standard 5 – Research

Students read to locate, select, and make use of relevant information from a variety of media, reference, and technological sources.

❏ Locate specific information using glossaries, alphabetical or numerical arrangement of topics, keyword search, and electronic media.

Directions: Use this index to answer questions 1–5. Darken the circle for the correct answer to each question.

Animals, alpine: altitudinal adaptation of, 107, 108, 110, 112, 114, 117, 119; domesticated, 122, 132, 134: hibernation of, 110–111

Asia: famous mountains of, 179

Boone, Daniel, 136, 137

Brazilian Highlands, 44

Earth's crust, 34; changes in, 9–10, 35, 36, 60–61 (see also Mountain building); continental vs. oceanic, 40, 58

Fiords, carving of, 48–49

Flowers, alpine, 84–85, 86–87, 89

Glaciers, 14–16, 24–27, 46; categories of, 16

1. Where will you find out about how fiords are carved?
   - Ⓐ page 44
   - Ⓑ page 50
   - Ⓒ page 46
   - Ⓓ page 48

2. How many pages have information on domesticated alpine animals?
   - Ⓐ eight pages
   - Ⓑ three pages
   - Ⓒ five pages
   - Ⓓ two pages

3. Which information would you read about first?
   - Ⓐ Daniel Boone
   - Ⓑ Brazilian Highlands
   - Ⓒ Alpine animals
   - Ⓓ Alpine flowers

4. If you read page 119, you will find information about ____.
   - Ⓐ Alpine animals' adaptation to altitude
   - Ⓑ Hibernation of alpine animals
   - Ⓒ Carving of fiords
   - Ⓓ Famous mountains of Asia

5. How many pages have information about glaciers?
   - Ⓐ four pages
   - Ⓑ five pages
   - Ⓒ ten pages
   - Ⓓ nine pages

Answers:
1. D, 2. B, 3. C, 4. A, 5. D

Standard 6 – Literature and Culture

Students read and recognize literature as a record and expression of cultural heritage.

❏ Read, respond to, and discuss a variety of literature as it connects to personal experience and cultural background.

Directions: For questions 1–4 read the selection. Then darken the circle for the correct answer to each question.

I think that some students are so afraid that they will fail a test that they panic. Their minds go totally blank. Then they feel that they have to cheat in order to pass. There are some other reasons that students cheat besides worrying about passing a test.

One reason is their parents. Some parents make their children feel that they'll only love them if they get good grades. Some parents even give their children gifts and money when they get high marks on their report cards. So what do some children do even though they don't feel good about it? They cheat.

Another reason they give for cheating is that sometimes students really don't understand the work. They're ashamed to admit that they didn't understand what the teacher said, so instead, they copy answers from people who sit near them.

Students who get away with cheating more than once can get into the habit of doing it all the time. Then they stop studying and count on other students to help them get by. I think that this is a bad habit to start.

1. Which would be a good title for this selection?
   Ⓐ How to Cheat on Tests
   Ⓑ Parents Want Students to Cheat
   Ⓒ Why Students Cheat in School
   Ⓓ How to Get Good Report Cards

2. What does the writer think parents should do?
   Ⓐ Stop giving children rewards for good grades.
   Ⓑ Love children only if they get good grades.
   Ⓒ Make children study more.
   Ⓓ Tell children not to panic.

3. What is one reason that students might cheat?
   Ⓐ They want to fail a test.
   Ⓑ They like to get gifts from their parents.
   Ⓒ They like to study.
   Ⓓ They have good habits.

4. What does the writer think about cheating?
   Ⓐ Everybody does it.
   Ⓑ It's a bad habit to begin.
   Ⓒ It's a way to get good grades.
   Ⓓ It makes your mind go totally blank.

Answers:
1. C, **2.** A, **3.** B, **4.** B

 MATH

Standard 1 –Number Sense

Students develop number sense, use numbers and number relationships in problem-solving situations, and communicate the reasoning used in solving these problems.

❑ Find least common multiple, factors, and greatest common factor.

Directions: For questions 1–8 darken the circle for the correct answer. Darken the circle for *Not given* if the correct answer is *not* given.

1. Which are the factors of the prime number 3?
   Ⓐ 1, 3
   Ⓑ 1, 2
   Ⓒ 3, 0
   Ⓓ Not given

2. What are the prime factors of 18?
   Ⓐ 2 and 9
   Ⓑ 3 and 6
   Ⓒ 2 and 3
   Ⓓ Not given

3. Which sentence shows 24 as a product of prime factors?
   Ⓐ $2 \times 3 \times 2 \times 2$
   Ⓑ $2 \times 3 = 4$
   Ⓒ 6×4
   Ⓓ Not given

4. Which is the greatest common factor of 8 and 12?
   Ⓐ 3
   Ⓑ 4
   Ⓒ 6
   Ⓓ Not given

5. Which are two factors of 12?
   Ⓐ 6 and 8
   Ⓑ 7 and 4
   Ⓒ 3 and 4
   Ⓓ Not given

6. Which is the smallest common factor of 8 and 12?
   Ⓐ 4
   Ⓑ 1
   Ⓒ 2
   Ⓓ Not given

7. Which are the least common factors of 6?
   Ⓐ 3 and 3
   Ⓑ 0 and 2
   Ⓒ 2 and 3
   Ⓓ Not given

8. Which are the common multiples of 3 and 4?
   Ⓐ 6 and 8
   Ⓑ 8 and 12
   Ⓒ 12 and 16
   Ⓓ Not given

Answers:
1. A, **2.** C, **3.** A, **4.** B, **5.** C, **6.** B, **7.** C, **8.** D

Standard 2 –Patterns and Algebra

Students use algebraic methods to explore, model, and describe patterns and functions involving numbers, shapes, data, and graphs in problem-solving situations and communicate the reasoning used in solving these problems.

❏ Recognize that a variable can represent an unknown in an equation, and apply in simple problem-solving situation.

Directions: For questions 1–2 darken the circle for the correct answer.

1. What number does y represent?

    $6 \times \boxed{y} = 42$

    Ⓐ 7
    Ⓑ 8
    Ⓒ 9
    Ⓓ 6

2. What letter should be in the box to make this number sentence true?

    $(a \times b) \times c = a \times (\boxed{} \times c)$

    Ⓐ a
    Ⓑ x
    Ⓒ b
    Ⓓ c

Standard 3 –Statistics and Probability

Students use data collection and analysis, statistics, and probability in problem-solving situations and communicate the reasoning used in solving these problems.

❏ Calculate averages using whole numbers and decimals.

Directions: For questions 3–4 darken the circle for the correct answer.

3. The Bennett family invited 15 guests for Thanksgiving dinner. The turkey cost $16.50, and the pumpkin pies cost $14.20. About how much will they spend on each guest for turkey and pumpkin pie?

    Ⓐ $30.60
    Ⓑ $19.20
    Ⓒ $2.00
    Ⓓ $31.60

4. Every afternoon Kelvin unpacks cartons and stocks the shelves in the Good Food Market. On Monday he stocked 30 cans of dog food, on Tuesday he stocked 25 boxes of cereal, on Wednesday he stocked 40 cans of tuna fish, on Thursday he stocked 35 boxes of cookies, and on Friday he stocked 55 bags of nuts. What is the average number of food items that Kelvin unpacked and shelved in one day?

    Ⓐ 45
    Ⓑ 49
    Ⓒ 37
    Ⓓ 39

Answers:
1. A, **2.** C, **3.** C, **4.** C

Standard 4 – Geometry

Students use geometric concepts, properties, and relationships in problem-solving situations and communicate the reasoning used in solving these problems.

❑ Know and be able to describe the properties and vocabulary of plane geometry (including lines, line segments, rays, angles, polygons, circles, parallelism, perpendicularity, congruence, and similarity).

Directions: For questions 1–6 darken the circle for the correct answer. Darken the circle for *Not given* if the correct answer is *not* given.

---

1. Which triangle has a line of symmetry?

Ⓐ A
Ⓑ B
Ⓒ C
Ⓓ Not given

2. Which of these is an obtuse angle?

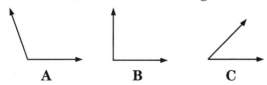

Ⓐ A
Ⓑ B
Ⓒ C
Ⓓ Not given

3. Which pair of lines is perpendicular?

A **B** **C**

Ⓐ A
Ⓑ B
Ⓒ C
Ⓓ Not given

4. Which shapes are congruent?

A **B** **C**

Ⓐ A
Ⓑ B
Ⓒ C
Ⓓ Not given

5. Which of these name parallel line segments?

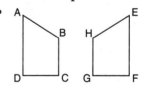

Ⓐ AB and CD
Ⓑ HG and EF
Ⓒ DC and BC
Ⓓ Not given

6. What is the measure of angle CBD on this protractor?
Ⓐ 120°
Ⓑ 90°
Ⓒ 45°
Ⓓ Not given

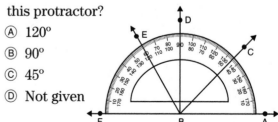

Answers:
1. A, 2. A, 3. B, 4. C, 5. B, 6. C

© Steck-Vaughn Company

Parents' Guide to Testing, SV 1311-0

Standard 5 – Measurement

Students use a variety of tools and techniques to measure, apply the results in problem-solving situations, and communicate the reasoning used in solving these problems.

❏ Use formulas to calculate the perimeter and area of squares, rectangles, triangles, and circles.

Directions: For questions 1–5 darken the circle for the correct answer.

1. What is the perimeter of this figure?

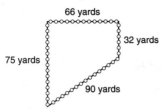

66 yards
32 yards
75 yards
90 yards

Ⓐ 360 yards

Ⓑ 220 yards

Ⓒ 263 yards

Ⓓ Not given

2. What is the area of this triangle?

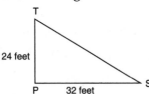

T
24 feet
P   32 feet   S

Ⓐ 68 sq. ft.

Ⓑ 128 sq. ft.

Ⓒ 768 sq. ft.

Ⓓ Not given

3. What is the perimeter of this figure?

Ⓐ 36 inches

Ⓑ 12 inches

Ⓒ 28 inches

Ⓓ Not given

h
← 6 in →

4. One of the trees in the Crane's backyard adds $\frac{1}{2}$ foot to its circumference each year. It is about 3 feet around now. Ray and his friends decided to guess what the tree's circumference would be in 10 years. Giselle thought the circumference would be 8 feet, Carlos thought it would be 5 feet, Benji thought it would be 13 feet, and Ray thought it would be 6 feet. Who do you think is right?

Ⓐ Ray

Ⓑ Giselle

Ⓒ Carlos

Ⓓ Benji

5. The Adams family is building an enclosed run for their dog. The run will be 75 yards long and 15 yards wide. What will the total number of feet in the perimeter of the run be?

Ⓐ 180 feet

Ⓑ 1,125 feet

Ⓒ 540 feet

Ⓓ 270 feet

Answers:
1. C, **2.** D, **3.** D, **4.** B, **5.** C

Standard 6 –Computation

Students link concepts and procedures as they develop and use computational techniques, including estimation, mental arithmetic, paper and pencil, calculators, and computers, in problem-solving situations and communicate the reasoning used in solving these problems.

❑ Demonstrate proficiency of converting fractions to decimals and percents.

Directions: For questions 1–6 darken the circle for the correct answer.

1. Which of these percents equals $\frac{4}{25}$?
   - Ⓐ 4%
   - Ⓑ 25%
   - Ⓒ 16%
   - Ⓓ 18%

2. Which of these decimals equals 36%?
   - Ⓐ 0.36
   - Ⓑ 03.6
   - Ⓒ 30.6
   - Ⓓ 36.00

3. Which fraction equals 12 $\frac{1}{2}$ %?
   - Ⓐ $\frac{2}{8}$
   - Ⓑ $\frac{3}{4}$
   - Ⓒ $\frac{1}{4}$
   - Ⓓ $\frac{1}{8}$

4. What is the fraction for 32%?
   - Ⓐ $\frac{5}{8}$
   - Ⓑ $\frac{32}{100}$
   - Ⓒ $\frac{32}{50}$
   - Ⓓ $\frac{10}{21}$

5. Change $\frac{2}{3}$ to a percent.
   - Ⓐ 33 $\frac{1}{3}$ %
   - Ⓑ 37 $\frac{1}{2}$ %
   - Ⓒ 66 $\frac{2}{3}$ %
   - Ⓓ 43 $\frac{3}{4}$ %

6. Round $\frac{13}{14}$ to a whole number percent.
   - Ⓐ 14%
   - Ⓑ 13%
   - Ⓒ 93%
   - Ⓓ 39%

Answers:
1. C, **2.** A, **3.** D, **4.** B, **5.** C, **6.** C

SCIENCE

Standard 1 – Physical Science

Students understand common properties, forms, and changes in matter and energy (with a focus on physics and chemistry).

❑ Measure quantities associated with energy forms (for example: mass, temperature).

Directions: Darken the circle of the correct answer to each question.

1. The production of heat or ___ shows that a chemical reaction has occurred.
   Ⓐ mixtures
   Ⓑ light
   Ⓒ dark
   Ⓓ scraps

2. Work is measured in
   Ⓐ pounds.
   Ⓑ seconds.
   Ⓒ meters.
   Ⓓ joules.

3. Geothermal energy is produced
   Ⓐ by the Sun.
   Ⓑ by the wind.
   Ⓒ inside the Earth.
   Ⓓ through lightning.

4. Appliances with higher wattage ratings
   Ⓐ cost more to run.
   Ⓑ are less expensive to run.
   Ⓒ need fuses.
   Ⓓ fall apart sooner.

Answers:
1. B, **2.** D, **3.** C, **4.** A

Standard 2 –Life Science

Students understand the characteristics and structure of living things, the processes of life, and how living things interact with each other and their environment (with a focus on biology, anatomy, physiology, botany, zoology, ecology).

❏ Categorize organisms according to their roles in food chains and webs.

Directions: Darken the circle of the correct answer to each question.

1. A food ___ describes how food energy is passed from one organism to another.
   Ⓐ market
   Ⓑ ad
   Ⓒ chain
   Ⓓ link

2. A food ___ shows all the food chains in an environment.
   Ⓐ poster
   Ⓑ web
   Ⓒ chain
   Ⓓ pyramid

3. These animals eat other animals.
   Ⓐ carnivores
   Ⓑ herbivores
   Ⓒ fungi
   Ⓓ producers

4. The relationship between living things and the nonliving environment is an
   Ⓐ omnivore.
   Ⓑ ecosystem.
   Ⓒ episode.
   Ⓓ accident.

Answers:
1. C, **2.** B, **3.** A, **4.** B

Standard 3 – Earth and Space Science

Students understand the processes and interactions of Earth's systems and the structure and dynamics of Earth and other objects in space (with a focus on geology, meteorology, astronomy, oceanography).

❑ Understand that changes in the atmosphere produce different forms of weather.

Directions: Darken the circle of the correct answer to each question.

---

1. The layer of air closest to the Earth is the
   Ⓐ exosphere.
   Ⓑ ionosphere.
   Ⓒ stratosphere.
   Ⓓ troposphere.

2. A twisting, funnel-shaped storm is a
   Ⓐ squall line.
   Ⓑ hurricane.
   Ⓒ tornado.
   Ⓓ blizzard.

3. A stationary front can cause an extended period of
   Ⓐ eclipses.
   Ⓑ precipitation.
   Ⓒ hurricanes.
   Ⓓ drought.

4. The average weather of a place over time is its
   Ⓐ biome.
   Ⓑ global warming.
   Ⓒ climate.
   Ⓓ temperature.

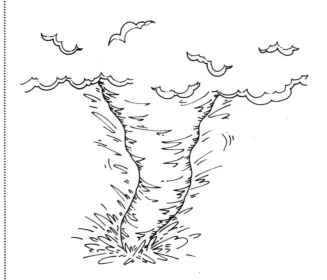

Answers:
1. D, 2. C, 3. B, 4. C